SHANGHAI LOSSES

ADRIENNE TROPP

A Lucky Bat Book
Shanghai Losses
Copyright ©2022 by Adrienne Tropp

ISBN: 978-1-939051-18-9

Cover Artist: Sarah Katreen Hoggatt
Published by Lucky Bat Books
10 9 8 7 6 5 4 3 2 1

DEDICATION

For Simon and Benjamin,
and all who agree with their sentiments:

Five-year-old Simon's note "I Wish For A Better World"
Posted August 13, 2018, at Renwick Gallery's
Burning Man Exhibit

I think about a world where only kindness exists.
I imagine a world with peace and balance.
There aren't any wars, only peace
People aren't mean and bullies are just a fantasy.
The only weapons are plastic toys.
Homeless people are never ever turned away.
Everybody shares and has equal rights.

Eight-year-old Benjamin's poem, "What I think about
when I recite the Amidah," written in December 2021

CONTENTS

PART 1

THE NEWS
OF THE DAY

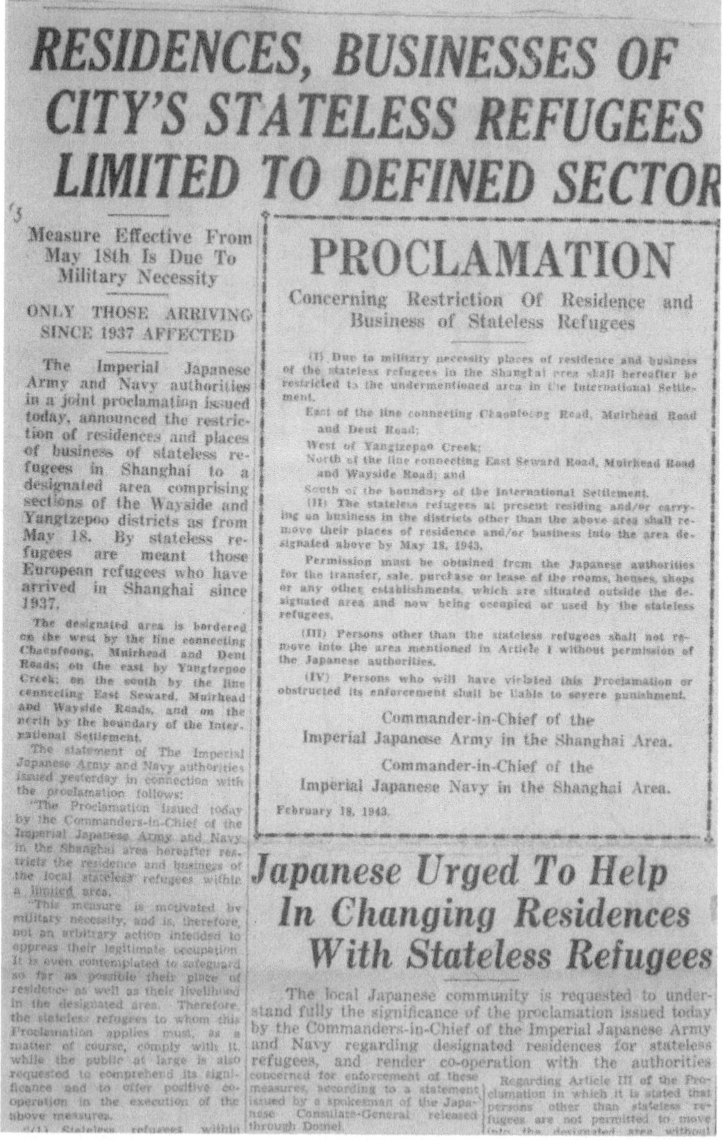

RESIDENCES, BUSINESSES OF CITY'S STATELESS REFUGEES LIMITED TO DEFINED SECTOR

Measure Effective From May 18th Is Due To Military Necessity

ONLY THOSE ARRIVING SINCE 1937 AFFECTED

The Imperial Japanese Army and Navy authorities in a joint proclamation issued today, announced the restriction of residences and places of business of stateless refugees in Shanghai to a designated area comprising sections of the Wayside and Yangtzepoo districts as from May 18. By stateless refugees are meant those European refugees who have arrived in Shanghai since 1937.

The designated area is bordered on the west by the line connecting Chaufoong, Muirhead and Dent Roads; on the east by Yangtzepoo Creek; on the south by the line connecting East Seward, Muirhead and Wayside Roads, and on the north by the boundary of the International Settlement.

The statement of The Imperial Japanese Army and Navy authorities issued yesterday in connection with the proclamation follows:

"The Proclamation issued today by the Commanders-in-Chief of the Imperial Japanese Army and Navy in the Shanghai area hereafter restricts the residence and business of the local stateless refugees within a limited area.

"This measure is motivated by military necessity, and is, therefore, not an arbitrary action intended to oppress their legitimate occupation. It is even contemplated to safeguard so far as possible their place of residence as well as their livelihood in the designated area. Therefore, the stateless refugees to whom this Proclamation applies must, as a matter of course, comply with it, while the public at large is also requested to comprehend its significance and to offer positive cooperation in the execution of the above measures.

"(1) Stateless refugees within

PROCLAMATION

Concerning Restriction Of Residence and Business of Stateless Refugees

(I) Due to military necessity places of residence and business of the stateless refugees in the Shanghai area shall hereafter be restricted to the undermentioned area in the International Settlement.

    East of the line connecting Chaufoong Road, Muirhead Road and Dent Road;

    West of Yangtzepoo Creek;

    North of the line connecting East Seward Road, Muirhead Road and Wayside Road; and

    South of the boundary of the International Settlement.

(II) The stateless refugees at present residing and/or carrying on business in the districts other than the above area shall remove their places of residence and/or business into the area designated above by May 18, 1943.

Permission must be obtained from the Japanese authorities for the transfer, sale, purchase or lease of the rooms, houses, shops or any other establishments, which are situated outside the designated area and now being occupied or used by the stateless refugees.

(III) Persons other than the stateless refugees shall not remove into the area mentioned in Article I without permission of the Japanese authorities.

(IV) Persons who will have violated this Proclamation or obstructed its enforcement shall be liable to severe punishment.

Commander-in-Chief of the
Imperial Japanese Army in the Shanghai Area.

Commander-in-Chief of the
Imperial Japanese Navy in the Shanghai Area.

February 18, 1943.

Japanese Urged To Help In Changing Residences With Stateless Refugees

The local Japanese community is requested to understand fully the significance of the proclamation issued today by the Commanders-in-Chief of the Imperial Japanese Army and Navy regarding designated residences for stateless refugees, and render co-operation with the authorities concerned for enforcement of these measures, according to a statement issued by a spokesman of the Japanese Consulate-General released through Domei.

Regarding Article III of the Proclamation in which it is stated that persons other than stateless refugees are not permitted to move into the designated area without

Figure 1: Announcement of Proclamation

February 18, 1943

I AWAKEN. SOMETHING'S DIFFERENT. IT'S QUIET. Too quiet. No breakfast plates clatter. No fish sizzles. No coughing from Momma. Anna's bed is empty, the sheets crumpled.

I clutch Mary and take a few steps from my bed. My eyes dart around the apartment. No one is here.

I shiver.

Opening our front door, I smell no food cooking, and I hear no shouts to hurry up nor sounds coming from the other apartments. *Has everyone left? Have I been forgotten? But Momma and Poppa wouldn't do that, not after all we've been through.*

"Mary," I say, "what should I do? Should I wait? Should I go to school?" Of course, Mary says nothing.

Momma would tell me what to do.

I dress for school and head toward the door. I go back. I take a few steps and turn again to glance around the apartment. Nothing has changed. Momma and Poppa still aren't here. Being by myself is scary. Heading to school makes sense.

I kiss Mary goodbye. I go back and give her another kiss. Her body, in its soft pinafore, presses against me. I hold her for a moment and rub my hand through her short hair colored a lighter shade of blond than mine. I decide today is a good day to take her to school with me. Will my classmates laugh? Mary has never attended school, not even while hiding in my satchel.

Stepping outside our building, I still sense something's wrong. The rough wheels of rickshaws click against the road. Dogs yelp. The foul smell of honey pots fills the air. Bodies lie near doorways. All this is usual, and yet it's not.

It's then when I realize I don't see refugees. I don't see children hurrying to school. I don't see men scurrying to work. No yentas stand in front of the building, whispering the latest news. Hesitantly, I head to school.

Only a few students and my teacher are present.

"Rachel, did your Momma and Poppa want you to come today?"

"Professor, I don't see them this morning," I say in my imperfect English. I rub my hand along Mary's head. I'm sure no one can see her in my satchel.

"You didn't? Hmm, I'm surprised. Go home. Wait for them," she says with her hands on my back. I move in the direction she's pushing me. "They may be worried if they don't find you there. Since early this morning, people have been discussing today's news about the Proclamation."

"What is proclamation?"

"Surely, your mother and father will explain everything when you see them."

I walk home slowly, taking baby steps like in the game I play with friends. I say to Mary, still in English, "That was school. Not so good. We get thrown out."

I don't want to worry Mary, so I don't say anything more. Something is wrong, and I'm not sure I want to know.

Three Years Earlier

T HREE YEARS EARLIER, ON A HOT, muggy September afternoon, I raced home with what I thought was the best news. I pictured how excited Momma would be when she heard what I had learned at school. This news I was to tell her, we had waited so long to hear.

I rushed past the yentas, knocking into one of them, who grabbed my arm and demanded an apology. I mumbled something to get past her and yelled, "Momma!" as I flung open the door to our second-floor apartment.

"Momma!" I screamed. "We can go to America! We can go! Today I learned!" I thought my news would make Momma so happy.

"Yes, bubbeleh, tell me and stop jumping around," Momma said as she sipped her afternoon tea.

Momma usually spoke to me in German, not Yiddish. I glared at her. When she called me *bubbeleh* instead of Rachel, I had either done something wonderful or I was in trouble.

"There's a Statue of Liberty in the harbor of New York in the United States of the Americas," I blurted out. I saw a few tears on Momma's cheek. Though she hadn't heard my news yet, I thought her tears were those of happiness.

"Our teacher told us today about it. This statue tells if we're hungry and tired we can go to America. Listen, Momma, listen, I learned some of the words." I proudly translated the English words into German.

Give me your tired, your poor,
Your huddled masses yearning to breathe free,
The wretched refuse of your teeming shore.
Send these, the homeless, tempest-tost to me,
I lift my lamp beside the golden door!

"You've said we're poor and you're tired of all this and we have no home. The poem on the statue says America wants us. Hear that, Momma? America wants us!"

As Momma stirred her tea, I could see her carefully considering my good news. After a moment, she moved closer. She held me and ran her fingers through my hair before she pulled back to look at me with her blue eyes. People who knew her when she was a little girl said I looked just like her. I wondered how true that was, with my hair cut so short and Momma's being curly and shoulder length.

She said, "Yes, you're right. Such a statue exists, with that poem by someone called Emma Lazarus. What nice words they are, but not words for us. They are not words for everyone."

Momma didn't make any sense. I took a step back.

"Don't look at me that way. Your sister recited the same lines when she started at the Shanghai Jewish School."

They knew about this statue and those words, but we didn't leave for America. Why?

Momma swallowed hard. "Your Poppa and me, we tried to go to America. We tried so very hard. We applied for visas, but they never came. America has what they call 'quotas.' Only a certain number of German Jews were allowed to come. We were given a number and told to wait. We waited. We

began to feel too afraid and didn't want to wait any longer."
I didn't know this.

"Now our home is here in Shanghai, and we are together."

"Why didn't you go somewhere else?"

"No country wanted us. No country lifted its quotas for Jews to enter."

"China did."

"No, not even China. It's complicated, and I don't understand." Momma stared at her cooling tea. "Japan invaded China a few years ago, and the Chinese areas of Shanghai came under Japan's control. Neither the Chinese nor the Japanese would issue visas, at least not for Shanghai. When we heard we didn't need one, Grandpoppa left for Shanghai. And you know we followed a few months later. We just didn't feel safe in Berlin any longer. People were acting *meshugana,* crazy, like jackasses."

At first, Momma received some letters from friends and relatives who stayed. Anna had sneaked a look at them, and she told me how much harder life had become for Jews still in Germany. The Germans charged Jews for the cleanup after the broken-glass night. Children could no longer attend school. Jewish shops were shut down. Jewish doctors could only treat Jewish patients, and Jews could not see non-Jewish doctors. Jewish people were sent away on trains and could take only one small case each, unlike the steamer trunks we took. That was the Germany we left behind.

"Grandpoppa had been right; Shanghai had been a good place for us," my sister Anna had said after reading Momma's letters.

Momma said, "Shanghai has been nothing like Germany. Germany spit on us; Shanghai welcomed us."

Momma only meant that we don't fear being Jewish here. She hates everything else, especially being sick all the time.

Things Fall Apart

M<small>Y THOUGHTS SNAP BACK TO TODAY</small>, February 18, and this proclamation thing. The day feels very different with so few refugees going about their business.

Maybe Shanghai is not so good anymore.

I go into our apartment. Momma, Poppa, and Anna are not home. "Mary, it's still the two of us. Professor thought we'd find them all at home."

As I put my satchel on the table, I spot *The Shanghai Herald*, the English paper Poppa buys for Anna and me to read. A German paper is there beside it, but I can't read German. There in the Herald in all capitals is the word: PROCLAMATION. I read slowly.

School is conducted in English. Few refugees knew any before coming to Shanghai. At first, I had sat in class just looking around. Only at recess did I hear any German. The teachers would yell, "English! Speak English!" After almost four years, I use English all the time at school and with friends. I still haven't learned some of the words I see in today's newspaper like *stateless, restriction, designated, establishments, situated.* Because it's written in capital letters, I know "proclamation" is something important. *Proclaiming* has to do with some kind of announcement. Below the headline, it reads, "Concerning Restriction of Residence and Business of Stateless Refugees."

Are we "stateless refugees"? I know we're refugees, but stateless? I hope not. The proclamation sounds scary.

As I continue reading, I learn stateless refugees must move to an area between Chaoufoung Road, Muirhead Road, and Dent Road, west of Yangtzepoo Creek. Where are these streets? I look at the wall as if it has an answer.

The names sound familiar, but I can't figure out why. I don't think they are in the French Concession, where we live, nor near the Shanghai Jewish School in the International Settlement, where I attend school; both areas are now controlled by the Japanese.

Further on, I read that stateless refugees who work and live "outside the area designated" must also move their businesses by May 18, 1943. That's three months from today. Will our family need to move? Does Poppa have to move his business?

There is more to the article, but I skip to the end: "Persons who violate the PROCLAMATION or obstruct its re-enforcement shall be liable to severe punishment."

Re-enforcement is a new word. I try to figure out the meaning from its parts. *Severe punishment* are two words I've heard enough of at school.

I'm frightened. Where are Momma and Poppa? Is Anna with them, or has she gone to help the rabbi's wife, whom she calls Rebbetzin. It's not like Anna to leave her bedsheets crumbled up.

I look again at the article and wonder if we could be jailed. Or will we be forced to go to internment camps, like the Americans and Englishmen did when America joined the Allies in the war? I don't know if any children were sent to the camps; I think they went back to where they were from as the war with America started. What is my home country? Will I go back to Germany?

The yentas tell all who listen of the horrible insect-infested camps around Shanghai. They tell of how the Japanese imprison anyone who still has a British or American passport. "How could this happen?" they moan.

I hear the yentas whisper that people in the camps have nothing to eat. I hear them tell of people becoming very sick and dying. I hear the yentas tell about Mr. Jameson, who worked for a British bank and was badly beaten. I hear of how he was returned to his home, where he lies unconscious to this day. "The horror of it," they say.

I know I shouldn't listen to them, but I'm pulled toward them. I want to hear their news.

And the yentas always have news. A few days after the Japanese bombed American ships, the yentas frantically told of an American lady who had just come to Shanghai. She was sent with lots of money to help struggling Jewish refugees. She, they told us, was imprisoned in one of the camps. America and their people are now the enemy of the Japanese.

As I reread the article in the *Herald*, I look for the word *Jews*. Is *stateless refugees* another way to say *Jews*?

While I stare at the paper, Poppa finally comes home, with Momma trailing behind him.

"Play outside for a while," Poppa orders me. "We'll explain what's happening a little later. Have some fun."

"Have fun," is Momma and Poppa talk for when they don't want me to listen to their conversation.

But I have a right to know what Momma and Poppa are keeping from me. I should know the truth instead of what they might make up for me. I thump down the stairs, slamming both the door to our apartment and the one to the building. Quietly, I reopen the outside door, tiptoe upstairs, and put my ear to the keyhole.

"Nobody said anything at the meeting!" Momma yells. "We're stateless and must go to a restricted area. Restricted area. It's a ghetto, that's what it is. They're forcing us into a ghetto."

Momma sounds angrier than I have ever heard her, even more than when Grandpoppa was taken prisoner on that night that changed everything. She's more upset than she was about Grandpoppa's death.

I don't want to listen to what she's saying.

I'm scared. I leave.

Natasha is waiting outside for me, as though she knew I'd come out.

She's my best friend. We share everything, even the bad things we hear from grownups or from other children. We've wondered how the yentas come by their information or how much of their incredible news could be true. We are almost like twins. "Two blond-haired, blue-eyed dumplets," Grandpoppa called us when he first saw us together. Natasha's momma said, "Amazingly alike, you two. Same foods. Same games. Same books."

Natasha knows more about what's happening today than I do. She tells me that anyone who left Germany, or an area occupied by the Germans, after 1937 is considered stateless and will need to move. "My family doesn't because we came from Russia a long time ago. Momma said your family will probably go to the designated area."

"Where is it?"

Natasha shrugs. We both know that the Yangtzepoo Creek separates where we live from other parts of Shanghai.

As we walk, down the street, Natasha and I puzzle out where the area is. After a few minutes, we figure it out.

It's the area called Hongkew, where many of the poorer Jews settled when they arrived in Shanghai. They live in Heimes, the homes set up for them. Also, lots of Chinese are crowded in there among bombed-out buildings. It is the worst area in Shanghai.

We agree it doesn't make sense for the Japanese to send more Jews to live in the area. People there are already crammed together.

"That's not so bad," I say, "not after coming all this way to Shanghai. At least we'll be living across the river from each other. We'll still see each other at school."

"Rachel, you've seen Hongkew."

I didn't want to talk about it. She knew I had been to the area.

Natasha and I hug.

"You'll see," she says. "Everything will be fine. We'll still see each other at school and on weekends."

It's not going to be too bad. It can't be.

I think about the area. I realize Grandpoppa took Anna and me there on adventures when we toured the city after we arrived.

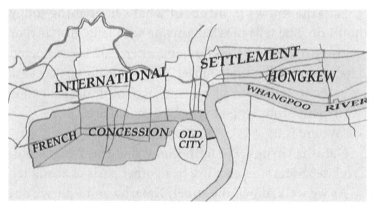

Figure 2: Map of areas of Shanghai

It wasn't as nice there as in the French Concession, where we had our first apartment. Will our apartment be even smaller than the one Grandpoppa had for us when we arrived? Even smaller than the one we live in now, where we moved after America went to war with Japan.

No, I think, *my family won't be moving there.*

Momma still talks about living in Berlin, with the beautiful Oriental rugs and crystal chandeliers. I don't remember much since I was six, when we left. Some places in Shanghai are as nice as Berlin had been, but not Hongkew. No wonder she's so upset about moving there.

Nothing is as good as when we first came, especially not since America entered the war. Momma and Poppa don't go to Roy's Rooftop Café once a week anymore. They don't go to nightclubs, cabarets, operettas, concerts, dramas, or the Yiddish theater since Grandpoppa died and the Americans left. Momma so loved the entertainment she had in Berlin.

I liked the quiet when Momma and Poppa were out for the evening. I didn't have to listen to Momma complaining about how much better Berlin was and how she wants to return to Germany. But best of all, Momma wasn't around to yell at me and tell me what to do. I think about how Shanghai was when we arrived, and I'm not paying attention to Natasha's comments until I realize she's become quiet. We're back at the front of my building. I start to open the door.

Natasha quietly says, "Don't go yet."

She stands on the sidewalk still saying nothing as I move closer to her to hear what she wants.

When I glance at her, I notice a frown and her scrunched-up eyes. She seems to be debating something. She blurts out, "You know what my momma called the designated area? She called it a ghetto and spit when she said the word."

"Ghetto! My momma used that word too! And she made it sound like something horrible. What's a ghetto?"

"I thought it was just a section of a city where lots of Jews lived," Natasha says. "But from the way my momma spoke the word, it sounds like a bad place. I'm probably wrong. We'll find out."

We say goodbye, and I walk upstairs slowly.

I listen for voices. I hear nothing and open the door. Momma and Poppa stand on opposite sides of the room, facing away from each other. They've had a fight. At the faint sound of the closing door, they both turn to face me but remain quiet.

I stand by the door, unsure what to do. I say the first thing on my mind: "What's a ghetto?"

"A place you should never know about. Our families moved to Germany over sixty years ago to avoid this," my momma says.

"Tell her," says Poppa. "She's going to find out. Remember, the paper doesn't call it a ghetto."

"Call it paradise, but it will mean the same thing. A ghetto, Rachel, is a place where they lock up Jews and won't let them out."

"A prison?" My voice quivers. If ghettos are bad places, why haven't people put a stop to them? Forcing people to live in one place because of who they are isn't fair. The people at the Heimes in Shanghai live there because they are poor; no one forced them to be there.

"Just about," she answers. "It means we can't live here anymore, and Poppa can't work here anymore."

Poppa hasn't been working much anyway, so it shouldn't make a big difference. Most days he goes off somewhere.

I ask lots of questions. Momma keeps answering, "How should I know? How should I know? Go ask the Japanese."

Momma and Poppa are upset.

Our family doesn't talk at supper, except for Momma asking Anna, who's home for our evening meal, "Are you all right, bubbeleh? Are you sure?"

Outside, the yentas discuss the proclamation. I hear snatches of conversation. The word *ghetto* comes up again and again.

People ask, "Will you move?"

"Is it really that bad in Hongkew?"

They repeat the same information over and over until it seems there is nothing more to say. People trickle inside for the night.

While listening to them, I comb Mary's hair. Anna yanks her from me, pulling out some of her short strands. "Don't you care what's going on? Look at you, playing with a toy. You're not a baby anymore. Start acting your age."

I stare at Anna, and I hug Mary. *You're my bestest friend, along with Natasha. I can play with you whenever I want.*

I remember the day Poppa took me to Peter Pan, the toy store on Joffre, the most beautiful street in all the French Concession. Carved wooden toys and cream-colored porcelain dolls just like the ones Anna had in Berlin filled the shelves. Mary was a present on my seventh birthday. I picked her out because she looked a bit like me, and I thought Natasha would like her too.

The family celebrated with ice cream later that afternoon. The five of us had sundaes at The Chocolate Shop. From its thirty-one flavors, I chose the Chocolate Shop Temptation. Even the Pineapple Coconut Sundae, which sounded terrible but had a fluffy cream topping and cherry, looked delicious.

Then we strolled through the park and watched people taking their birds for a walk. The bamboo cages they held swayed from side to side and songbirds chirped from within. That day was one of my happiest in Shanghai.

I felt sad later that night when on the way home I saw Chinese workers in Peter Pan unfold their sleeping rolls in the loft above where they worked. *They sleep there!* I thought. *Don't they have homes to go to? That's terrible!*

Anna comes to me later this evening. So much has happened today because the proclamation has been issued. Life will be different.

She kisses my forehead. "I'm sorry, Rachel. You are acting your age. I guess I'm hoping this nightmare will end. We've been through so much."

The street empties, and Anna and I ready ourselves for bed. I fall asleep quickly, but later I am awakened by Anna's screams. "No, no, stop. STOP!"

I sit up. Anna is having another bad dream. "Leave Poppa alone. Stop! Our dishes. Poppa! Grandpoppa. Why are they taking him? *Please*, don't!"

Anna is dreaming again of that dreadful night. I go to her side and try to wake her.

"Anna, it's okay," I say to her as she awakens. "We're not in Berlin."

Momma comes running. She holds Anna tightly, smoothing her long, dark hair and wiping tears from her freckled face. "It's okay, bubbeleh. Everything will be okay." She holds Anna until she falls back to sleep.

I know what her nightmare is about. I remember the day, even though I was only six.

Jewish storefronts were smashed, and synagogues wrecked and burned. Grandpoppa and many others were taken away. Poppa ventured out very carefully to look for him and learn what he could. Momma, Anna, and I waited anxiously and spoke in hushed voices. When Poppa returned, he had no news. On the street, glass crunched under the boots of SS troops.

Anna's seventeen, so I thought her nightmares had gone away, but I guess she's not too old to have them. Her nightmares began as we traveled by boat to Shanghai, but she hasn't had one in months.

As usual, Anna sleeps more peacefully the rest of the night.

MOMMA'S GONE

A MONTH HAS PASSED SINCE I READ about the proclamation. Moving day is getting closer, but we don't have a place to move to.

In the meantime, Anna doesn't have any more nightmares. She seems to be calmer, more accepting, almost happy. Her reaction is strange considering what's going on.

Momma is absorbed in her own world and has been since the proclamation.

Momma does less each day. It's as if, since the proclamation, she has wilted like a flower out of water. She hardly leaves the apartment. She doesn't prepare meals nor help clean. She doesn't notice messy papers or crumbs on the floor. She stares at Grandpoppa's picture and babbles. I'm unable to understand what she's saying. She's a different Momma than I've known.

I think Momma is even more upset about Grandpoppa's death now than when it happened. And he wasn't even her poppa. She had met him soon after her own died when she was nine. Grandpoppa had given her momma a job and checked on how the two of them were doing. When Momma was fifteen, her own momma died, and Grandpoppa had invited her to stay with his wife and him. They were like foster parents to her. She moved out of their house after she began earning a living. They kept in close contact. Momma had always felt very close to them and married their son. Momma liked to tell Anna and me, "The Weisers saved my life. They were so kind to my momma and me. I don't know what would have happened to us without them."

I have noticed that Poppa, too, seems different somehow. He comes and goes as he always has. He makes sure we have enough to eat. He brings home the noon rations from the Jewish Distribution Center (JDC). Each day he sends our *amah*, or housemaid, to the market to purchase food, though it's never enough to fill our bellies. Many nights he brings home scraps of food. Poppa has brought home chunks of bread, a cooked vegetable mash, rice mixed with I don't know what, boiled potatoes, a piece of a Viennese cutlet, shreds of beef, and, once, a large slice of a torte, or cake, with raspberry filling. Anna and I always hungrily grab for the tiny pieces of meat. We gobble up our portion of the torte. Such food is wonderful to have. After a few days, I realize he looks worried.

The only time I asked Poppa about the food, he said, "Be thankful for what you have been given and do not question. Others are not so fortunate."

It was the kind of voice that says, "Don't question me!"

Momma and Poppa and Anna go on as if no proclamation has been posted. I'm the only one in the family who seems concerned about what will happen on May 18.

Hongkew's Rooms

MY SCHOOLMATES TALK ABOUT THE ROOMS their families have found—ugly, small, dirty, bug-infested places. They talk about horrible smells. They talk about dead bodies on the street.

A few weeks after February 18, Lillian says to Dora, "I heard your mother found a good place."

"It's only good because we have a flush toilet in the building," Dora says. "My cousin, who will be living with us, said the building used to be a Chinese school."

Another schoolmate complains that he will be living with his grandmother, aunts, uncles, and cousins, all in one room.

I can't imagine how they will do it. Will they sleep standing up?

Everyone seems to be finding places to live.

My family hasn't even started the search.

One night just before dinner, I blurt out, "Momma, aren't you going to look for an apartment?"

"Leave Momma alone. Just leave her alone!" Anna yells at me. "Moving is hard. Finding a place is harder. You don't need to remind her." Anna leaves the apartment after her outburst. Even Anna is acting strangely.

I'm not ready to forget about the proclamation. Somebody must do something before it's too late.

I talk to Mary about the problem. She's a good listener, and she never snaps at me.

Later that evening, I ask Poppa, "Doesn't Momma need to look for a place?"

"It's not up to you to question your momma, but just so you know, she and Anna plan to look next week."

Anna returns in time to hear Poppa's words but doesn't add anything.

Momma ignores our conversation. She holds Grandpoppa's picture to her chest and, as usual these days, mumbles words I don't understand.

Another week passes. I'm more worried. Aren't people going to be jailed if they don't move? Is my family going crazy?

I say to Momma, "Poppa said you and Anna would look for an apartment. Have you?"

"Yes. Yes," she answers vaguely. Momma isn't listening. I don't know what to do. Anna and Poppa aren't around much these days, and neither seems to be concerned.

Again, I ask Poppa what's happening. "My school friends talk about places their families have already found."

Momma overhears me. "You want one of those places so bad, tomorrow, I take you. Then we'll see how bad you want to move."

The next day, we cross the Garden Bridge into the designated area. A Japanese soldier hits a Chinese man who is balancing a bamboo pole across his shoulders with a bucket hanging from each side. Chickens squawk from inside the baskets. An egg falls out of one of the baskets. The soldier kicks the man, and he topples over. The soldier yells something at the man while pointing at the mess.

He's probably ordering him to clean it up, but I doubt the Chinese man understands the words. The man, trembling, uses his tattered clothing to wipe up the egg.

"Momma, did you see?"

Another man limps across the bridge, and another soldier points the tip of his bayonet at him.

"Momma!"

Momma pushes me forward ahead of the man, muttering, "Just worry about you. It's a big enough job."

Hongkew stinks like a giant bathroom. I didn't notice it as much when Grandpoppa toured us around. People jam together in lanes too narrow for a car to drive down. Chinese women cook over flowerpot-looking stoves. The smell of rotten fish and food fills the air. A ragged child crouches on the ground holding his leg, which has green pus oozing from it. A baby wrapped in newspaper is pushed up against a door, not moving. I realize after a moment that it's dead. Tears fill my eyes to see people living so terribly.

"So have you seen enough?" asks Momma. "And you want to know why we haven't found a place to live in Hongkew."

"It's bad, but don't we have to move in six weeks?"

Momma doesn't answer.

Later, I visit Natasha and describe what I saw. Natasha's mother, who speaks and understands a little English, listens intently.

"Some Russians helping search," she says and has Natasha write down a few names and their contact information for me to give to Momma.

I arrive home with the note from Natasha's mother and translate it into German. Momma and Poppa argue a bit, but Poppa likes the idea of having a Russian help. "The Russians," says Poppa, "have been good to refugees like us,

Figure 3: View of the Garden Bridge

Figure 4: Aerial view of Shanghai

Figure 5: Inside a lilong (lane)

and they've been in Shanghai for many years. Though, of course, they are not as rich as the Baghdadi Jews, like the Sassoons and Kadoories, but they have been generous."

"Natasha's momma says they speak some English. Either you or Anna will need to translate for Momma," Poppa says as he puts down the note.

Poppa seems to be reading the note, which is in English, but Poppa can't read English. I wonder how he figured out what Natasha wrote, even before I translated it. Some English words are like German ones. Maybe that helped.

I volunteer to go with Momma, and the next day we set off for Hongkew again.

Momma has her list of what she is looking for. I translate for Mr. Feldman, the Russian she chose to help us. "Musts," he reads. "Running water, a flushing toilet, a kitchen, electricity, and an icebox. Bedroom for Momma and Poppa."

Looking at Momma, Mr. Feldman says, "You rich, very rich? Then we can find such a place or fix up one. Some of the bombed-out buildings can be renovated. How much do you have to spend?"

When Momma has me tell him the amount, Mr. Feldman laughs. "Tell your momma maybe we can find a bathroom for that amount or a closet you can all squeeze into."

After many hours of looking at terrible places, I say, "Momma, we cannot find what you want. You see what the man has shown us. I think the second one off Chusan Road is best. At least it is large enough for us each to have a bed, and for a table. The building has a bathroom."

I should know better than to tell Momma what to do, but she doesn't scold me.

"A bathroom that is not private is no good. And flushing toilets… there aren't any," she says. "We saw only those so-called honey pots that need to be emptied every day. We cannot live like that. We are civilized. We are Germans! No good! Absolutely no!"

Momma refuses to accept the situation. She can't have what she wants. In the past, she often had her own way. When we arrive home, Poppa is waiting. Momma walks past him without a word. She sits in the corner, her arms folded, her eyes staring at Grandpoppa's picture. It's as if she's asking him for help. She had been very fortunate for his help her after her momma died. Now Momma must fend for herself.

Poppa turns to me. "What happened?" He glances at Momma sitting in the corner in a kitten-like ball covered by a blanket.

I describe to Poppa the rooms we visited, tell him the rent amounts and how much the key money would be. I know about key money from listening to classmates. Their parents don't understand the idea. I only understand that people must pay a large amount of money in addition to the rent for a place. I tell Poppa so.

"We will take the one you say is best. We can pay the amount wanted. At least the room will hold the essentials, and we'll manage. I've heard how bad it is there."

Poppa and Mr. Feldman agree on the arrangement and Poppa signs the papers.

We will move soon. We won't face jail.

The next day, I describe the place to Natasha. "Oh, it sounds terrible," she says and hugs me. "Terrible. What are you going to do?"

Natasha's mother, Mrs. Rabinovich, stares past us and says, "Rachel and her family do fine. They strong. Make good bad situation."

I might have believed that before the proclamation, but since then Momma forgets to even wash or get dressed.

Sometimes she doesn't even eat. How will our family adjust to our new situation?

I tell Natasha that after we move, Anna and I will need to share a single bed. We've never shared before. "She gets home later and later. She claims it's because she puts the children to bed and then plans the next day's activities and meals with the rebbetzin. She'll awaken me when she climbs into bed."

"Do you really think she's talking with the rebbetzin that late? Anna's pretty. I bet she has a boyfriend."

"Anna with a boyfriend? That's funny."

Natasha and her mother begin speaking in Russian. They almost never do that when I visit. I hear them mention my name. Natasha nods and says, "*Dah, dah.*" Yes, yes.

As she often does, Mrs. Rabinovich sends me home with leftovers from tiffin, the large, delicious lunch Russian families eat. "I make too much," she says, "enough to feed half Shanghai. What thinking, was I? No room icebox so much. Favor, take home." Her family doesn't need rations.

Because we have barely enough to eat since the Japanese and Americans are at war, I'm happy to have more food.

I thank Natasha's mother and start toward home. "Rachel," calls Mrs. Rabinovich before I am gone, "let mother and father know we talk come evening."

Natasha, as she often does, translates her mother's words into better English. "Momma and Poppa want to talk to your parents this evening."

They are coming to my house! Will they tell Momma that they send food home with me? I carry home the package, but today I don't eat from it as I often do.

The evening turns out to be busy.

PART 2

CHANGES ARE COMING

VISITORS IN THE NIGHT

THIS NIGHT, ANNA COMES HOME TO eat supper with us. She announces that one of the rabbis from the Mir Yeshiva would visit later.

"But please, Poppa, don't say what you usually do about the yeshiva. This rabbi, he's not like the others. He cares about all the Jews, not just the yeshiva students."

"Oh, so he's come to tell me he will share the extra food the students and rabbis get? No, no, I think he will tell me that the students will exchange their nice rooms with those living ten to a room in Hongkew."

"Poppa, please, for me, be nice to him," Anna pleads.

"For you, my *shayna*, I'll try to behave."

The Jews in Shanghai know the yeshiva students spend their days studying. The yentas have reported the kosher meats they obtain and plentiful vegetables they eat while most of us almost starve.

"Those poor students and their teachers," Poppa has said, "traveled across Russia and eventually ended up in Shanghai. So did those poor Polish Jews, who arrived with nothing and have nothing." Poppa has expressed his opinions before. He feels that the yeshiva students have more than a fair share of what's available to other refugees and receive larger payments.

I wonder if Poppa will really behave for Anna.

But my worry is what Natasha's mother will say to Poppa and Momma. But maybe, now…

After dinner, a rabbi and a student knock on our door. Both are dressed in black jackets and pants, white shirts, and black hats. They look just like the rabbi whose wife Anna works for, but unlike many of the other yeshiva students who are in Shanghai.

Usually when I see some of the more orthodox men, I giggle at their full beards, their curly sideburns, and their long coats in the heat of Shanghai. They look out of place compared to the other men. The youngest students have the beginnings of their beards. Always, I see the knotted white fringes of their prayer shawls hanging from beneath the coats of the religious men. These two who are at our door don't look like them.

The rabbi asks to speak to Poppa. Anna and I leave.

"That's one of the Mir Yeshiva students with the rabbi, isn't it?" I ask Anna.

She nods.

I can't think of why they would need to talk to Poppa unless another family wants Anna to work for them and they need Poppa's permission.

I wonder if the student with the rabbi is one of those who took part in the riot. The yentas told how the yeshiva students acted when the proclamation was issued. They refused to move to Hongkew, with the rest of us. They smashed tables and chairs, broke windows, and threw objects out the window of the office where people were helping them find housing. Poppa spoke about their terrible behavior. He thought it reflected poorly on the rest of us.

"You know what Poppa says about those Mir students. He says they are self-centered and selfish."

Anna walks away from me. I know Anna has food to eat at the rabbi's house, and she never brings any home. "It's not fair."

Anna turns to me. "You don't know anything. They do God's work. They're good people. They follow the teachings of our faith, unlike—" She stops.

"That boy. He's your boyfriend. Anna has a boyfriend," I say, suddenly realizing it. Natasha was right. Anna has a boyfriend.

"That shows how little you know. Mir students don't have girlfriends. They spend their time studying." Several times, Anna glances at the front door and turns away. About twenty minutes later, the men depart. They bow to Anna. I look more closely at the younger one. His clothes are too large for him and hang down as if someone dressed a stick. The boy seems a little older than Anna. They leave without saying a word to her. The boy doesn't see Anna's small wave. They continue down the street and Anna darts upstairs to our apartment.

"Well," says Poppa, "I have had the most unusual request." He looks at Anna. "So, you already know?"

"I pray you agreed, Poppa."

"Is this what you want?"

"Yes," Anna answers.

I have no idea what they are talking about.

At that moment there is a knock on the door. "Do you think they have changed their minds?" Poppa winks at Anna.

Mr. and Mrs. Rabinovich and Natasha are at the door. I forgot they would call on us tonight.

Poppa welcomes them and calls to Momma that we have visitors. I hear noises from the other room; Momma must be dressing and fixing her hair for this unusual visit. Most days, she remains in her sleeping clothes. Everyone talks about the warm April weather while they wait for Momma. Natasha translates from Russian into English, and I from English to German. It's slow, but no one is saying anything important.

When Momma comes out from her room, Natasha and I are told to go downstairs.

"What's going on? Your mother has never come to visit before," I ask Natasha.

"You'll never guess. It's so exciting. Mother and Father want to adopt you. We'll be sisters and you won't have to move to Hongkew."

Adopted. Not live with Momma and Poppa and Anna? Not live in that horrible place we're moving to in a few weeks? Have enough food?

"Won't it be great?"

"Yes," I say, though I'm not so sure.

"Natasha, Rachel, please come in," calls Poppa from the window a few moments later.

"I assume Natasha told you what I come discuss. You and Natasha always sharing secrets. This too big to keep." Mrs. Rabinovich turns back to my parents. "I hope you all will give suggestion thought. We are serious. Rachel is like part of our family already. As I said, some people are doing these temporary adoptions. We want make life easier for Rachel and you, Mr. and Mrs. Weiser."

Russian, Yiddish, German, English—translations fly about, making it hard to understand what's happening.

Turning to me, Mrs. Rabinovich says, "We have space and want care of you, Rachel. No live like the Sassoons and Hardoons in big houses, but you no stand on the food lines. Only 'till this crazy goes."

After the Rabinoviches leave, Momma says quietly, "My children both want to get away from me. What have I done?

Haven't I been a good mother? Haven't I always given to my children? Anna wants to get married, and to a religious Jew. I knew taking that job would come to no good."

Anna married. So that's what the visit was about. The marriage was arranged in the proper way. The stick boy hasn't really been her boyfriend, not like in the books where they kiss and things. But Anna has been preparing. Since she started working for the rabbi's wife, she has been mumbling prayers in Hebrew before and after eating. She no longer eats certain foods, even if it's all we have. Once she wouldn't eat a tiny bit of meat with cheese.

When I asked her why, she said, "My tastes have changed. They cook differently at the rabbi's house, and I guess I'm used to it now."

Momma's sharp voice disturbs my thoughts. "And you," she says pointing a finger at me. "You traitor, you. You help us find a place and all this time you were plotting to get away."

"No, Momma, I had no idea why the Rabinoviches were coming over. I thought I was in trouble, that I had done something bad at Natasha's."

"That food you brought home today, I should have thrown it to the rats. It was a bribe. You wanted me to see how well the Rabinoviches could take care of you."

"No, Momma! No!" It is no use. Momma doesn't listen to anything. Who will make the decision about where I will live? Anna has a say in her future life. Will I? Will Momma and Poppa?

Important Decisions

MOMMA IS IN HER OWN WORLD. Anna spends all her time helping the rabbi's wife with her four young children. Poppa is gone all the time. Why should I stay? It will only be worse when we move to Hongkew. Momma has told me to thank the Rabinoviches for their generous offer, but she will not allow them to adopt me. Maybe she thinks back to when both her parents died, and she was "kind of adopted." It's not like that because I'll see Momma and Poppa all the time.

Maybe another reason she won't let me live with the Rabinoviches is that Momma may feel she'll need me at home even more once we move. Or maybe she wants to see me miserable.

Momma must change her mind. I haven't told the Rabinoviches that Momma has made a decision because I intend to move in with Natasha's family.

I continue to spend most of my time at Natasha's. One day, Mrs. Rabinovich says, "Rachel, almost like you our family member." She switches to Russian and Natasha translates. "Your momma seems to be letting you spend more time at our house. She's curious. Is your momma trying to adjust to what it's like when you're away?"

I gulp and smile.

The truth is Momma thinks I'm helping Anna. Lucky for me, Anna doesn't say anything.

Together Natasha and I have been plotting. We come up with ideas so Momma will feel she won't need me around.

At home, I don't do what I'm asked to do. "Rachel, what's with the rice? Why is it scorched? How do you expect us to eat this?"

I feel bad. We have so little to eat, and I'm making it worse.

I reply, "Rice is hard to make. You've even said so. I guess I'm just not good at it."

Momma makes no reply but eyes me strangely.

Another time, I forget to hang up laundry. "Rachel," Momma says, "why is your uniform rolled into a ball? It won't dry that way. You know better."

And yet, another time, I tell Momma that my ration card was stolen. I came up with that idea on my own. "Rachel!" Momma screams. "Now we'll have less to eat!"

"I couldn't help it. I couldn't fight that big guy. He looked like he was in high school." I had even bruised my arm to make it look like someone had attacked me. "You don't even care that I'm hurt."

Momma says nothing.

I had thrown away my ration card. I knew I could always get something to eat at Natasha's. New cards would be issued in the next few days. I am careful with Momma and Poppa's cards.

"Who needs you? You're only causing more work around here!" Momma shouts one evening after I knock over my bowl of watery stew.

Good, the plan is working.

Poppa looks at me. "You're asking for a beating. Start making yourself useful."

I wipe the food from the floor but leave the dirty towel on the table.

"You know where the garbage is. Throw that filthy thing away," Momma snaps.

"You're always yelling at me. You hate me. Why don't you just get rid of me?"

Momma and Poppa both look at me.

"So that's your plan," Poppa says. "You want us to throw you out. Then you can go live with Natasha's family. If you do, you'll be dead to us."

Momma takes a deep breath.

"No," I protest feebly.

"Go, I don't want you around anymore. Where are the papers? I'll sign them. Just go!"

"Calm down," Poppa says to Momma.

"Go live with the Rabinoviches. What *chutzpah*!"

"I think maybe Momma has a point," Poppa says. "Things are hard enough without you adding to them."

I leave the house and sit on the front step for a few minutes. I've heard those words before. According to Momma, Grandpoppa used the words, "You are dead to us," when her sister-in-law had married a gentile, a non-Jew. He threw her out of the house and never talked to her or saw her again. As he lay dying, several months before the Japanese bombed the Americans, he told the family he regretted not seeing Beatrice again. "Families should be close no matter what."

Heading to Natasha's, I think of what I should say. I don't think Natasha's mom would allow me to live with them if she knew what happened.

"Good news," I say after the walk to her house. "Momma and Poppa have agreed that your family can adopt me." Lowering my voice, I say, "Natasha, our plan worked."

But Mrs. Rabinovich overhears me. "What plan?" she asks. She stands in front of us with her hands on her hips and her feet apart. She wants an answer!

I look to Natasha. She shrugs her shoulders.

Mrs. Rabinovich continues to stand before both of us. "You two have plan so parents agree?"

"No," Natasha says.

"No! No! Of course not," I say.

Mrs. Rabinovich turns to Natasha. "Truth, Natasha. Now!"

Afraid that Natasha will tell her mother the truth, I quickly say, "The plan was only that I would spend more time here. Then Momma could see she doesn't need me."

"No, plan was make everything easier you and family. You good friend Natasha," Mrs. Rabinovich says coolly.

Now I have angered Natasha's mother. It seems I won't be welcomed anywhere.

Where will I sleep? Will I live like the children I see on the streets, begging for food and wearing tattered clothing? Will I have to eat scraps from the garbage? What can I do now?

"Natasha, you stay. Rachel and I go her house now."

"No, Mrs. Rabinovich. I can't go home. My parents don't want me."

"No choice."

On the way to my parents', I confess to Mrs. Rabinovich. She takes me in her arms and says, "Everything work out. Don't worry. Parents love you."

I doubt they love me anymore.

When my father opens the door, Momma walks away. "This ungrateful child is no longer welcome here. And you, a parent, should be ashamed of yourself!" she shouts in Yiddish.

"Please, hear me," says Mrs. Rabinovich. "Rachel, please, outside."

I obey and don't listen through the keyhole. What will I do? It seems forever before Mrs. Rabinovich appears. When she does, she says, "Everything fine. Go now. Remember, hurt parents. Long time to right. Next days, no see my Natasha."

THE MOVE

WE LOOK AT OUR BELONGINGS. WE can't take most of them with us. We try selling the clothing, toys, cooking items, and furniture we have no room for. Poppa says, "Everyone is selling. Few people are buying."

Momma just sits while Poppa and I pack.

Moving day arrives. We say goodbye to the only Jewish family left in our building. They too will move in a few days. Poppa hires two rickshaw drivers to move our things. I am to run alongside one of the drivers, and Poppa will meet us at our room. Momma will stay at the old apartment, watching as our possessions are loaded up in the other rickshaw. Anna promised to help but she's not around. Her new Judaism applies only to the Mir Yeshiva and its families.

Poppa puts our mattresses on one rickshaw and leaves ahead of us. As the rickshaw driver hurries along, I keep a hand on our two thin mattresses and run alongside the cart. I see other stateless refugees running alongside rickshaws, keeping their eyes on the few possessions they have. The rickshaw drivers pass through the crowd like a rat through a maze. One of our mattresses begins to topple as we round a corner. I can't let it land on the filthy streets. I shove it back

Figure 6: House belongings moved by rickshaw

but meet resistance. "It's okay, Rachel, I have it," calls Anna from the other side. Anna has come! She carries on her arm a small basket I don't remember seeing before. I also see Stick and another yeshiva student running alongside our rickshaw. My eyes tear up. Anna hasn't forgotten us, and she brings help. I worried about how I would be able to watch all our household goods. I know Poppa has only partially paid the workers until they arrive at our new home, but I feel our household things are worth more than their wages. I remember Poppa's words: "Few people are buying."

As we reach our destination, I'm exhausted and think about how hard a rickshaw driver's life is. Once I arrive, the plan is for Poppa to finish helping Momma.

A tiny Chinese girl watches us as the rickshaw is unloaded. Her dark eyes bulge from her thin body. Will she try to steal something? I watch carefully.

Later, Momma and Poppa appear, riding in yet another rickshaw along with the second one containing the rest of our belongings. We take turns unloading our few possessions. I can't believe how much smaller the room is than I remembered.

Yakov, the yeshiva student, and Stick find seven men on the street to form a minyan, along with them and Poppa. Yakov nails a four-inch rectangular bamboo box at a forty-five-degree angle to the right side of the doorpost. The ten men recite a blessing.

My show-off sister asks if I know what was nailed to the doorpost.

"I'm not an idiot," I answer. "It's a mezuzah."

"Only the rolled paper inside is a mezuzah," she answers.

Yakov says, "I wrote it myself observing the proper rules. It's my first time writing one. Rabbi says I did an excellent job." He turns red and bows his head. "Do you know where the words come from?" he asks nicely.

Embarrassed for not knowing the correct answer to Anna's question, I come up with the only thing I can think of. "The Torah."

He smiles at me. "Yes, you are right. The words are from Deuteronomy."

After we have moved everything inside, Yakov says, "We have a surprise for your family."

"Yes, today, no rations," says Anna. "The rabbi's wife prepared food for us."

We sit on the beds in our small place, unable to offer chairs to our guests. Momma, Anna, and I sit together, and the yeshiva boys sit with Poppa on the other bed. Even with all this food, we have less to eat than what we had when we first arrived in Shanghai. It is much more, though, than we've eaten at one meal in months.

I put a piece of meat in my mouth and chew it, savoring the perfect blend of spices. "This is as good as cook made in Berlin," says Anna.

The rice pudding is moist and chewy. Momma says, "That's almost the way I remember it in Germany."

The bread, challah, is baked well, with a crunchy crust I like. I eat every bit and regret it. When will I eat like this again? Maybe if I had gone to live with Natasha... Or maybe if I marry a yeshiva boy.

No wonder Anna is marrying Stick, whose name I learn is Schlomo. A thought strikes me. Did Anna bring Yakov to meet me? Is she trying to arrange a marriage for us one day? I turn around to look at Yakov, but the men's backs are to us.

I hadn't looked at him closely before. He seems much older than me. He has dark hair and is thin but not skinny like Stick. That's all I see. Yakov seems nice.

My mind wanders. *What would it be like to marry a rabbi*? I shiver. I have no idea of the kind of husband I'd want one day but being a rabbi's wife sounds hard. There's too much to learn, too much responsibility.

They leave, and I'm not able to see Yakov's face.

The little Chinese girl is squatting outside by the door. Maybe I should have shared some food with her. How ridiculous—she probably wouldn't like our food.

Anna spends the night. The room is barely large enough for the two beds. She screams out in her sleep. "Leave me alone! Stay away!"

I feel the same way as bugs crawl over me and swarm about. Momma doesn't help her; she knows she can do nothing.

Slowly, we adjust to our new space. Momma and I learn to use the flowerpot to cook our foods. We sit outdoors at night to avoid the heat in the house. Men and women strip to their underwear in the summer heat. Women chat; we see the Chinese women do this too. Men smoke and play cards, and we hear tiles click as the Chinese men sit around a table playing a game called mahjong. I don't understand the rules, but I watch the fast-paced game that uses small, square tiles with what seem to have Chinese characters. The men argue and bet small pieces of candy. The men's games are exciting to watch. I begin to understand some words the men use: *ee, are, san.*

We only talk with others like us since we can't speak Chinese, and the Chinese don't speak German, Yiddish, or Polish.

Each morning, I stand in line to fill a thermos with hot water from the water vendor. Momma seems more content. She talks to some of the women in the lane.

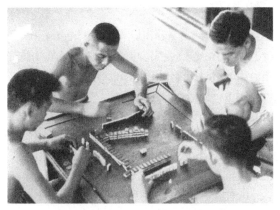

Figure 7: Playing mahjong

Figure 8: Heime

Figure 9: Street in Shanghai ghetto area in 1943

I'm miserable. What would life have been like if Natasha and I were together? I see her only at school. Life has also become harder for the Rabinoviches. Rarely does Natasha have any food to share with me.

I learn the Chinese girl with the large eyes is called Ling. At school, our Chinese teacher tells me it means "delicate." She does look like she could topple over. The dead children on the street, though, have ribs protruding from their chests. Ling looks better fed, but not by much. She continues to watch me. Outside, I play hopscotch by myself. Several days later, I notice Ling has made a hopscotch pattern with trash from the street.

I wave my hand for her to join me. She doesn't.

Anna visits regularly just to chat and help out.

A few weeks before the 1943-1944 school year begins, Anna brings me a jump rope made from pieces of cloth knotted together. She ties one end of the rope to a chair and swings the other so I can jump. Ling watches. After a few minutes, Anna turns to her and points to the rope.

Ling backs away.

Anna says, "Your new friend likes to hang around. Do you two play together?"

"No."

"Too bad." Anna hesitates, then she speaks quietly. "I came for two reasons today. I'm sorry, Rachel, I know you don't want to hear this, but I won't be able to visit for a while. Mrs. Kaplan is pregnant and having problems. The doctor wants her to stay in bed. She'll need constant help with the children.

"Also, I came to tell everyone that Schlomo and I will be married about six weeks after the Kaplans' baby comes. Rebbetzin Kaplan is helping plan the wedding." Anna's face glows as she talks about the wedding.

So, the rope Anna brought is a goodbye present. She won't be back. I can add Anna to the list of lost people I keep in my head. Holding the jump rope, I think back to Grandpoppa and Natasha, people no longer in my life—two of the people on my list. Then there are those like Momma and Poppa, who are lost in their own worlds. How long will this list grow? I don't want to think about them, but I do.

PART 3

MEMORIES OF GRANDPOPPA

After That Horrible Night

G RANDPOPPA'S LOSS WAS THE WORST BECAUSE it was the first. He made our move to Shanghai bearable.

Grandpoppa went to the hospital and never came back. When he was admitted, the doctor told Poppa, "It doesn't look good. The rest of the family needs to be careful. Mr. Weiser should have seen a doctor sooner. He's been sick too long."

"It wasn't until he had a high fever and was too exhausted to move that I made him come to the hospital. I wish I had realized sooner," Poppa tells the doctor.

"I think Grandpoppa knew almost immediately," Anna said. "He told me he thinks he ate some food and drank some water in Hongkew that didn't taste right."

"All the more reason, he should have been seen by a doctor. By the time a patient experiences exhaustion, the typhoid may be too far along. If any of the family or Mr. Weiser's friends or neighbors experience headaches, fever, or stomach pain, they need to be examined by a doctor immediately. We have a vaccine. It's been around for almost 30 years. People shouldn't be dying of typhoid fever anymore. Unfortunately, the supply in Shanghai is limited, but there's enough unless we have a major outbreak."

After we listened to what the doctor said, Anna sobbed, "It's my fault. I should have told him to see a doctor. He was already weak from the beatings he got in Berlin. He was never sick before then."

I didn't hear the doctor say that the beatings caused him to be sick. Could it be true?

I think about the time Grandpoppa was imprisoned. That was over two years ago, just before we came to Shanghai. For two days and nights in November, Jewish synagogues and businesses were destroyed. Germans ran through the streets, breaking windows of Jewish stores and stealing what they could. They set fire to the inside of synagogues and dragged out the Torahs, the scrolls with the first five books of the Bible and holy to Jews. Firemen stood by doing nothing unless a burning store was owned by a non-Jew.

The Gestapo stormed our house, smashing furniture and dishes. They were looking for men over eighteen. Grandpoppa came home just as they arrived. Poppa wasn't with him. Afterward, we heard many Jewish men had been arrested.

Momma and Poppa talked quietly after Poppa's attempt that night to find Grandpoppa. Momma journeyed out two days later to see if she'd have more luck. She learned he was in a nearby concentration camp.

To be released from the camp, the authorities needed proof that any imprisoned person had a way to leave Germany, not just Berlin. Momma ran about trying to procure train and boat tickets to anywhere outside Germany.

Early one evening, after a week of trying, she rushed in, waving something in her hand. "I've done it! I've gotten tickets. We can leave."

"How? Two days ago, you told us there were no tickets to anywhere," I said.

"I've learned that Italian liners to Shanghai will allow us to travel. And I've also bought both the train tickets to Genoa—that's where the ship leaves from—and the tickets for the ship."

"Where in America is Shanghai?"

"It's not America. It's China. Rachel, from there we can go elsewhere, maybe even America. We can't wait. Grandpoppa needs to leave as quickly as possible; otherwise, the police will keep him imprisoned. Grandpoppa leaves in less than two weeks, but I couldn't get tickets for the rest of us until April."

Momma said she'd been to Gestapo headquarters, where our tickets had been examined. Permission for Grandpoppa's release would be processed in the next forty-eight hours. Her happiness faded for a moment when speaking about her encounter with the police. Quickly, she regained her enthusiasm. "The first good news for us in a while. It sounds like a long time, but before you know we'll all be safe and together again."

On that terrible night when Grandpoppa had been dragged from the house, Anna and I had huddled together. She told me about a conversation she overheard among Grandpoppa, Grandmomma, Poppa, and Momma about two years earlier. They had discussed leaving Germany after the latest round of laws was passed. "Poppa and Grandpoppa were furious that they had to register their business. Grandpoppa feared more restrictions."

He urged Poppa to leave. Poppa said the worst had to be over. "You'll see," he told Grandpoppa, "German citizens won't allow these restrictions to continue. And we can't go anywhere until Grandmomma is better."

Anna continued, "Tonight proves how bad the situation has gotten. Poppa was wrong."

We all suspected Grandmomma's cancer had spread. We could see the increased pain she was in. Poppa seemed to be fooling himself about her diagnosis.

Grandmomma's condition worsened rapidly, and she died within a month.

"But I misunderstood what Grandmomma meant when she had said, 'Don't worry about me.' I had thought her comment referred to a new treatment the doctors had recommended and that it wouldn't be painful," Anna said. "That was wishful thinking on my part.

"A short time later I heard how concerned Grandmomma was for us," she continued. "'Jacob, be a *mensch*. You must do what is best for the family. Get out of Germany now. Don't procrastinate anymore.' She knew it was Poppa who was reluctant to leave."

On that night with Germans roaming the streets, windows being smashed, and uncontrolled fires everywhere, Anna was confiding in me. I didn't understand why.

I remember that after Grandmomma died, Gerta left. She had been our housekeeper for years.

Anna sounded like a know-it-all in revealing what she knew, especially about Gerta. She blushed slightly as she said, "Of course she had to leave. She wasn't forty-five."

I had no idea what Anna meant and what Gerta's age had to do with anything. Were younger workers needed elsewhere?

Anna told me that females in the households of Jewish families we knew were also forced to leave, but not those of my non-Jewish friends.

And why only some of the female workers? That is strange. Cook did stay until we left for Shanghai.

So much was happening around the time Grandmomma died. The events were horrible and didn't make sense. I was glad to have Anna around. We talked and shared news. Sometimes I wished Anna wouldn't tell me so much. She did take care of me almost as good as Momma, who liked to be out and about all the time. I became more worried about a week before that horrible November night. Momma was upset when she came home. From now on, she said, she preferred to stay home in the evenings. We never learned why.

Of course, I knew about certain changes, such as those on our passports. Momma and Poppa had talked about it. When our passports were returned, a large "J" had been stamped on the left side of the page, and our middle names had become longer— "Sara" was added for women and "Israel" for men.

"Still, even with the new passports and a request from his own mother, Poppa didn't want to leave." Anna eyes misted as she told me more, making that horrible night seem even worse. "He and Grandpoppa yelled, each calling the other, 'dummkopf.'"

Neither my easygoing sister nor Grandpoppa usually let things upset them, but now everything seemed to.

Before Grandpoppa was arrested, I noticed our sitting room and dining room furniture began to go missing. The boy downstairs said he was going to live in my apartment when we left. No one had told me we were going anywhere.

When I was around, grown-ups whispered. The whispering came more and more often.

Momma thought I was asleep when Grandpoppa came home from the camp on November 12, three days after his arrest. I peeked from my bedroom door. Through his torn pants, I saw scabs on his legs. His face was swollen and bloody. He wore no shoes or socks, and his feet appeared larger than usual. I tried not to cry. I didn't want Momma to know I was awake.

By morning, he looked better. He wore his robe and slippers. And maybe some makeup.

Grandpoppa left about ten days later for Shanghai. He looked mostly better.

He had been right. We should have left earlier.

THE SHOCK OF SHANGHAI

WHEN OUR BOAT DOCKED IN SHANGHAI that May, Grandpoppa was waiting for us. Many passengers boarded open trucks, but Grandpoppa had hired a car. *A car!*

In Berlin, we had ridden in a car only on special occasions. Once was when Grandpoppa's business received an award. Another time, Grandpoppa hired a car to take us from the synagogue to the cemetery when Grandmomma died. We rode in silence. No one mentioned that two of Grandmomma's closest friends who weren't Jewish hadn't attended her funeral.

We were happy to see Grandpoppa and ran toward him. He had left in November, which seemed so long ago. He greeted us with hugs and kisses. We gave him some of his favorite candy from his favorite sweets shop. The owner had left it in front of our door. He couldn't sell it to us since he wasn't Jewish. He had known Grandpoppa for years.

I stared at Grandpoppa. He wore regular shoes, and his pants were not torn. His face wasn't swollen. He looked like my regular old Grandpoppa!

He said, "Three weeks at sea! A three-week vacation with lots of activities. How wonderful for you, and on the *Conte Rosso*, such a beauty, and with delicious food and great hospitality. I felt like a very important person, a king at least, when I traveled here to Shanghai on the *Conte Rosso.*"

"Oh, Grandpoppa," I giggled, "you need a crown to be a king."

He laughed. "Oh, to be treated so well! And to feel safe and to relax were best of all. So many activities to keep all of you busy."

We shook our heads in agreement, and Anna said, "Well, Poppa certainly kept busy. We only saw him at meals and at bedtime."

To me it felt like we were at home, with him always working.

"I, for one, can't imagine what kept him so busy," said Momma. "Always running off to something, while in the evenings most of the women had their husbands at their sides to play cards and dance with. I spent the time by myself. That was not the way I imagined the crossing would be."

"Well," Grandpoppa said, "I'm sure Jacob had important things to attend to."

By the docks, I gagged on the smells around me. A boy urinated into the river from the side of what looked like a small houseboat. People threw trash and fish bones into the river from their boats. I had never seen anything like this before.

A new adventure was beginning. As soon as the car moved away from the docks, Momma muttered, "Oh, *vey iz mir*! What have we gotten ourselves into?" Over and over, she muttered these words until we neared our apartment.

I bounced up and down, looking out the car windows as best I could.

Along The Bund, where we had docked, Momma pointed out women who took nimble steps and wobbled on their feet. Something seemed wrong with them.

Figure 10: A view from Shanghai rooftops, 1945

Figure 11: Picture postcard of the port of Shanghai along The Bund,
1930-1937.

I said, "Momma, they look old. What could have happened to them?

I preferred instead to watch the beautiful young women, with their long, straight, black hair and long, colorful silk gowns with high collars, walking along quickly.

Men wore dresses, long dresses, also with the high collars, that were the color of mud. None of the men walked funny.

Some adults wore pointy straw hats tied under their chins. Their loose, dirty pants and tunic tops were smeared with dirt like my clothes when I played in mud. Flimsy straw sandals barely seemed to protect their feet.

Many men dressed in suits like those in Berlin.

I had never seen so much variety.

Bicycle bells clanked. Whistles blew. Street vendors called out in high-pitched voices. Car horns honked. I covered my ears but kept my eyes open. I was fascinated by the tangle of people and cars.

Wheelbarrows with passengers, rickshaws pulled by humans, handcarts filled with goods, people balancing bamboo poles with baskets on each end filled with food or blocks of covered ice were everywhere.

On our ride, we saw tall, turban-clad men with dark beards wearing khaki uniforms and blowing whistles to direct traffic.

It was exciting. It was scary. It was all so different.

The car stopped in an area Grandpoppa called the French Concession. He apologized for the small apartment. He said, "Shanghai has gotten crowded. It is hard to find places outside Hongkew where many of the refugees go."

Our new apartment was about half the size of the one we'd had in Berlin. Grandpoppa would share a room with Anna and me. He had put up a sheet to separate his space from ours. Momma and Poppa had their own bedroom. The kitchen had a sink, an icebox, and a stove. We had running water, a bathroom, and even a small entry to a living and dining room. I jumped when I heard the telephone. "Grandpoppa," I asked, "you have a phone? Can I talk on it?"

"You have a friend in Shanghai to call? By all means, go ahead," he joked.

We hadn't owned a telephone in Berlin, but Grandpoppa and Poppa had one at work.

He introduced us to the amah and houseboy he had hired to help with the cooking and household chores and to care for Anna and me. "I don't know what I would have done without their help."

I never saw where he and Poppa worked, but it was in the International Settlement. Many Americans lived there, and our school was there. Their business involved Americans in some way. "Learn English," Grandpoppa yelled at Poppa. "I can't be the only one dealing with our clients."

Grandpoppa's English wasn't too good either, as far as I could tell.

He and Poppa talked in hushed voices about work. Most of the time, I couldn't hear what they discussed. Once, I heard Poppa whisper that Grandpoppa's trick for hiding money and jewelry had worked well.

I wondered what they meant. Our train had been stopped at the German border, and we had been thoroughly searched. How could Poppa have hidden anything?

Explorations

GRANDPOPPA SEEMED HAPPY THAT WE WERE with him. We were glad to see him looking so good.

He spent time with me and Anna. "We will explore your new homeland. Tomorrow, I will begin by taking you to the famous Bund."

"Look at the buildings," he told us when we arrived there. "What do you see?"

"Big buildings and small buildings," I said. "And wide and narrow buildings."

He laughed. "My, you have a lot to learn." He rattled off words like "art deco" and "Renaissance." He looked at us and saw puzzled expressions on our faces.

"Ah, too advanced for my beautiful young granddaughters." He stood still for a moment.

"Look over there. Do you see the building with the four clock faces? That's the Customs House. You can see the clock tower from different vantage points around the city."

Then he pointed to the right. "Another building that's easy to pick out is the ten-story Sassoon House because of its green pyramid. It was built by the wealthiest man in Shanghai, and he's Jewish. Today, the bottom floor houses refugees."

Figure 12: The Shanghai Club   *Figure 13: Customs House*

Figure 14: Sassoon House

When we went inside the Sassoon House, I saw bunk beds and the sheets people hung with strings for privacy. "You two are very lucky," he told us. "Many refugees live in places like this, called Heimes, in Hongkew, an area of Shanghai. There you will see many Japanese soldiers."

"Japanese soldiers in Shanghai?" I asked.

"Yes. They leave foreigners alone. You're fortunate," he said as he pointed to the bunk beds, "that your poppa planned ahead so we could live well here."

Many men sat on beds and played cards. I didn't see any women or children.

Grandpoppa took us into the Shanghai Club. We weren't supposed to be there since it was only for British men. "Shh!" he said. "No talking. If they hear us speaking German, they'll know we're not English gentlemen."

We walked up to the second floor. Ignoring his own advice, he spoke. "See if you can figure out what makes this building famous."

Anna put her finger in front of her mouth and said, "Shh!"

Grandpoppa grinned. "You, good listener."

I don't think he really expected us to be quiet.

Not even trying to keep my voice low, I said, "The view of the river?"

Grandpoppa shook his head.

"The elevators," Anna and I called out at the same time, indicating the two of them side by side.

"Shh!" he said. "Do you give up?"

We did.

"See that bar?"

We nodded.

"That L-shaped mahogany bar is the longest in the world," he said.

A long bar. That was the big deal? Probably only to a grown-up.

Several times, he announced, "Park Day," and he took us to Jessfield Park. I loved walking around the pond but cried when we went to the zoo. I hated looking at caged animals. People and animals shouldn't be in cages.

On "Mansion Walk Day," he asked us to select a mansion for him to buy. He told us most were air conditioned and had swimming pools and beautiful gardens. All of them sounded wonderful to me. Even better than our apartment in Berlin.

Grandpoppa interrupted my thoughts. "But be sure, very sure. I wouldn't want to buy unless you're very, very sure. Moving can be so difficult."

"Oh, Grandpoppa, you're so silly," I said.

"I wish we could go inside," Anna said.

"No problem," said Grandpoppa. "We'll claim to be the new cleaning team."

"But Grandpoppa, we don't have any cleaning supplies."

"Rachel, you're such a worrier! They'll let us in because… because we're dressed so nicely."

"To clean houses, Grandpoppa? There's no way anyone will believe us," I said.

Homes of the Wealthy

Figure 15: European-style house

Figure 16: Spanish-style villa

Figure 17: Modern villa

Figure 18: English-style villa

Some Apartments in French Concession

Figure 19: Avenue Joffree

Figure 20: Haig Court

Figure 21: Gascogne

Anna smiled. "We'll have to be investigators. We're here to investigate the kind of rats they have."

"Settled then," said Grandpoppa.

On another walk, Grandpoppa said we were window shopping. "Make sure the window we buy can be hauled up the stairs," he teased.

"Grandpoppa, you've changed. In Berlin, you were so serious," Anna said.

"Berlin was a serious place."

We strolled along Nanking Road looking into the Chinese stores, which sold linens, silk, jade, and gold jewelry. We dreamed about what we would buy with a million yuan. Grandpoppa said, "I'd like that long, golden gown."

"Why?" Anna asked.

"Then everyone would think I'm Chinese."

"Grandpoppa, you're too tall for anyone to think that," I said, and we laughed.

As Anna and I pointed to things we liked, Grandpoppa laughed at us. "We don't have enough room for all that unless we find a second apartment, or maybe one of those mansions."

He bought us sweets at a chocolate shop and told us not to tell Momma, or next time he'd make us share with her.

Another series of walks he called, "The Fun Streets in Shanghai." Here, kids dodged about. Adults shuffled past. Amahs and houseboys jostled us as they ran errands. We strolled about, stopping to watch various sights. One day it was snake charmers and acrobats.

On another, we saw a parade with a long dragon. Grandpoppa told us to count the feet so we could see how many people were moving under the dancing dragon. It was hard to keep up with the moving dragon. Even though I could see people holding up the dragon, I couldn't count how many there were.

He pointed to the rear ends of little children. "Look!"

We giggled at seeing their pants slit in the back but agreed with Grandpoppa that it was a useful design.

Sometimes, we'd watch a funeral. Grandpoppa told us the crying women at the end were professional mourners. *How strange.* We learned the cymbals and other noisy music chased away ghosts. "Do you see any ghosts?" Grandpoppa asked.

When we told him we didn't, he said, "See how well it works."

Figure 22: Street acrobat

Figure 23: Chinese funeral procession band

I couldn't feel sad that someone had died because I felt I was watching a lively street play. That had been so different from the way I had felt after Grandmomma died. I couldn't stop crying for days, and people just kept hugging us and saying what a kind, thoughtful woman she was.

Unexpectedly, one day Grandpoppa said, "I think the time has come to buy you a Chinese business. We need to carefully check the possibilities."

For a few minutes we followed a barber who carried a small washbasin and a stool. Grandpoppa said, "What a great business! Look, he can take it wherever he wants."

We watched him set up, fill his basin with water from nearby, and begin work. After cutting one man's hair, he cleaned the scissors and washed the hair clippers in the dirty washbasin water. From a pouch, he pulled out a razor and shaved the man's face. The barber wiped the razor on a leather strap from time to time. Just as he was finishing up, he took a long bamboo stick from his pouch. It had a tiny spoon on the end.

"What's that?"

"Watch! You'll see."

He used it to clean out the person's ears!

"Grandpoppa, that's disgusting.

"Better than going around with waxy ears."

The barber finished with his customer, tossed the water on the ground, and moved on.

A shoemaker looked impressive with his various tools. "Another portable business," Grandpa said. "Look what he has there—hammers, nails, needles, leather, scissors."

I saw the shoemaker pull a foot form from his sack and place the customer's shoe on it. He ripped off the old sole, measured and cut some leather, and pounded in small nails.

He trimmed the leather some more until he seemed pleased with the result and returned the shoe to his customer. The man put his shoe back on, gave the shoemaker some coins, and wandered off.

"What do you think?" asked Grandpoppa.

Anna answered, "I don't think so. Did you see his fingers?"

The library we passed wasn't very interesting. Large wooden shelves held hundreds of books. People sat around reading. They couldn't move much because the books were attached to chains. I wondered how much people paid to sit on the stools, or maybe the payment was for reading a book.

"That's the one for me," I called out as we came to the next vendor. The man wore a long black robe with a round cap on his head. He was drawing beautiful pictures.

"How great! You've mastered both spoken and written Chinese," Grandpoppa joked.

"Huh?"

"He's a letter writer."

"Oh, I thought he was painting."

"The man on the stool tells the letter writer what to put down. When a return letter arrives, the letter writer will read the response. His fee includes that."

The scribe, as Grandpoppa called him, poured a few drops of water onto a dark square and moved his brush around in it. Then he applied the brush to the paper in front of him. I had seen Chinese writing on stores, but I had never seen anyone actually write. At first, I thought Grandpoppa was joking, but he was serious.

"I still think I'd like to learn how to do that."

"And maybe one day you will," said Grandpoppa.

Figure 24: Street barber

Figure 25: Shoe mender

Figure 26: Traveling children's library

Figure 27: Public letter writer

Figure 28: Cages with songbirds

We watched other workmen, and as it neared the time to return home, we went into what we had called an *apotheke* in Germany. I learned the shop sold traditional Chinese medicine. Behind a counter were small wooden drawers with Chinese characters written on them. Grandpoppa handed the man at the counter a slip of paper. *Der apotheker* didn't take anything from the small, ancient-looking wooden drawers behind him. Instead, he unscrewed several jars and grabbed items from a few baskets. He placed the mixture in a brass pan, removing some until it balanced with a weight hung on the other side. Then, with a mortar and pestle, he crushed everything until it became paste-like and gave this to Grandpoppa.

On the way out, I noticed containers filled with dried insects, fur, animal parts, roots, dried plants, and flowers. *How terrible.*

"What did you buy?" Anna asked.

"Just something to clear up a rash on my back. Either of you interested in owning a medicine store like that?"

"Yuck! I wouldn't touch those things," I said.

"It seems to me you two are very difficult to please, but we'll keep looking." He winked.

Figure 29: Traditional medicine shop (modern photo)

Many of the businesses by Nanking Road and Avenue Joffres, near where we lived, were more to my liking. In the windows, we viewed magnificent Chinese brocade robes, which Grandpoppa said were made from silk and were expensive. Anna wondered why the robes were long and the arms were always extended straight out. We had never seen anyone on the streets wearing anything like them.

Furniture, jade, and ivory—all hand carved—were sold in nearby stores. I stared at lacquered furniture, trays, and boxes. The shiny finish on them protected the detailed flower designs and scenery painted underneath. I never saw two that looked alike.

"I'd love a lacquered box, maybe for my next birthday," Anna said.

Grandpoppa told us that few people could afford the goods in these stores.

"Even us?" I asked.

"Possibly one or two of the less expensive jade or ivory items, but not the larger pieces. The Chinese have a long history and have perfected many arts. Maybe, after the war, we can bring back a nice Chinese memento or two."

From time to time, he told us a little about Chinese civilization. We learned about the Great Wall, which was built to keep out invaders. He told us about the Forbidden City, where the emperor and his family had lived. Commoners like us, he said, were not allowed to enter.

I had a hard time believing the Chinese had once had a great civilization. The streets here were disgusting. On many, I saw waste from both dogs and people. Grandpoppa told me that I shouldn't talk about it to other people. It wasn't nice manners. I could talk about seeing rotting fruit peelings, raw bones, dead cats and rats, rags, and lots of garbage. The streets in Hongkew always smelled bad, and I'd hold my breath.

Figure 30: View of traffic and shops on Nanking

Figure 31: Tramways and cars on Nanking Road

Figure 32: Commercial street scene

Figure 33: Crowded street

The French Concession was nicer. As we walked about, I realized Shanghai was becoming home to me. Few things surprised me anymore, and I loved seeing how differently the Chinese lived.

Best of all, there were no German soldiers to bother us on the streets. Japanese soldiers tended to bother the Chinese. The American, British, and French soldiers were usually friendly. They smiled at the children and stopped to talk. Sometimes, they'd have little sweets to hand out.

Those had been good days. Grandpoppa had helped us forget the horrors of what we had left behind and embrace the new world we had entered. Grandpoppa could feel comfortable anywhere. Anna was like him that way.

PART 4
GETTING HARDER

More Lost People

THEN GRANDPOPPA DIED. WE BURIED HIM in a plain
casket. Only about twenty people, including us, followed
his casket to the new cemetery on Columbia Road. A rabbi
gave a eulogy for him. He didn't tell how smart Grandpoppa
was, nor that he knew a lot about Shanghai, nor that he ran
a successful business. He did say that his family would miss
him. The rabbi was right about that—more than right.

The Chinese wore white for their funerals; we dressed
in black and read prayers. Our funeral seemed dead, like
the person it was for. I thought Grandpoppa would have
wanted a Chinese-style funeral with singing and dancing,
but I didn't tell Momma and Poppa that.

I cried, but only Mary knew. I told her I would never
see Grandpoppa again, that my life had a big hole. I wished
she could talk to me. I told her things I wouldn't even tell
Natasha, and she was my best friend.

Grandpoppa didn't live long enough to see how bad our
lives became. He had died about six months before Japan
bombed Pearl Harbor, in someplace called Hawaii, where
American ships were stationed.

It was bad enough that Grandpoppa was gone, but Poppa
went away, too, at about the same time. Well, not *really* away

like Grandpoppa, but he was hardly home. He disappeared like he had on the ship. That's when I began my list of lost persons.

Sometimes, I would see him hold something that had belonged to his father, and a few tears trailed down his face. After his father's funeral, Poppa never spoke about him. It seemed strange, but he had always been quiet, unlike his own poppa, though he looked like him.

He complained. "Bills, bills, bills. Not enough money."

"Jacob, you've always complained about bills, even before we came to Shanghai," Momma said.

"Since America is at war with Japan and Germany, we only have what we brought from Germany. It won't last forever."

"And neither will the war."

"Until then, though, we have two rents to pay, fees at the Shanghai Jewish School (SJS), the wages for the amah, and the houseboy, along with everything else."

If I couldn't go to the SJS anymore, I wouldn't have any friends. I had to go to school.

After the Japanese dropped bombs on the Americans, Anna told me Poppa had no work, and he didn't even pretend to go to his office. I wondered if I should tell Poppa he could save money by not renting office space anymore.

Poppa kept odd hours. He often took something with him when he went out. Once, he emptied Grandpoppa's trunk and dragged it away. That night when he came back for dinner, he put some coins on the table.

At first, he had only taken Grandpoppa's things; then he began taking his own clothing and some of his books. A few of Momma's pretty dresses disappeared. Some days he gave Momma money, but most days he didn't.

One day, he put more money than usual on the table.

Anna said later, "Things can't be too bad. We eat good meals and still have our amah and houseboy."

Within a week of Anna's comment, Poppa said, "We can do with less space now that my Poppa is gone. I've found a smaller apartment nearby. Rachel, you should be happy, it's closer to your friend Sasha."

"Natasha," I corrected, but he didn't seem to hear me as he continued.

"We'll still have two bedrooms, a kitchen, a bathroom, and a salon for greeting visitors."

Anna said to me, "Remember the Heime Grandpoppa showed us? There was no room between beds and people hung up blankets for privacy." I remembered. "We're fortunate in comparison. We'll still have a nice apartment, even if it is smaller than the one we're living in now."

Our family didn't know at the time that this wouldn't be our last move in Shanghai. When we arrived at the new apartment, we realized what Poppa hadn't told us. The beds in the room Anna and I shared were so close together, we bumped our knees getting out of them. He hadn't told us our dining table would be in the kitchen. We complained when we saw it. In comparison to the one room we would later have in Hongkew, this apartment was spacious, but at that time, we didn't appreciate it.

Worst of all, Momma learned our amah and houseboy were not coming with us.

When Momma realized she wouldn't have their help any longer, she became furious. "I can't live without them!" She threw pots and pans on the kitchen floor. "What do you expect me to do with these?"

"Momma, I'll help. Anna will help," I mumbled at the time, frightened by Momma's outburst.

I tried to sound brave, but I wasn't feeling that way.

Later, I had asked Anna, "Why did Momma throw the pots and pans?"

"In Shanghai, everything is different, and she probably doesn't know how to do much."

That night I thought more about what Anna said and realized maybe she was right. I knew Momma didn't know how to cook. Like most families who had lived around us in Germany, ours had a cook and a housemaid who would also look after Anna and me.

In Shanghai, our amah had been hired to shop and cook. Just as I had liked to watch our cook in Berlin, I'd peek over our amah's shoulder and watch her dicing and chopping washed vegetables. In Berlin, Momma never came into the kitchen except to give cook the menu.

I had watched our amah wash our fruits and vegetables multiple times in hot water and what Anna called potassium permanganate before they were cooked or eaten. She'd rinse the fruit until the pink color of the water disappeared. I watched her boil the fruits that had thin skins. We hadn't washed fruit in Berlin. I'd just pick up an apple and not worry about getting sick from it.

Sometimes when I didn't have school, our amah took me to the market. I felt like I was watching a show. Amah would hold up a piece of meat or some vegetable, make a face, and throw it down. She and the merchant argued. The merchant shook his head. Amah continued arguing. He'd respond. Then she'd nod, and hand him the money. She'd leave the market smiling. "Me do good." Around us I watched similar scenes.

The houseboy ran errands and kept our house clean, but Poppa insisted we couldn't afford to keep him.

In a short time, we lost Grandpoppa, our nice apartment, and our houseboy—more to add to my list. To make

Momma happy, Poppa let our amah stay, but we shared her with other families.

After our move to the smaller apartment, Poppa was home even less and became more distant. Momma didn't know where he went. One night, returning earlier than usual, he said, "Miriam, the news isn't good. Hitler keeps advancing. No one's seems able to stop him."

I wish Poppa would tell Momma the bad news when I'm not around. If Hitler wins, we won't be able to go back to Berlin, and everything won't be good again.

Poppa's thoughts were elsewhere. He stopped asking about school. He stopped asking Momma about her day or about news from the yentas. I noticed how he dragged his feet; he used to almost have a spring to his walk.

In February, when the proclamation was announced, Momma became lost in another kind of way than Poppa. She didn't talk to her friends anymore, nor to the yentas on the street. She didn't help with laundry nor patch our worn-out clothes; some chores she was forced to do when the houseboy left. She no longer used our nice tablecloth nor placed a single flower in our small crystal vase as she once had done. She didn't seem to care about anything.

Since we had arrived in Shanghai, Momma had always said, "Though we are in this depraved environment, we will continue to live like the civilized people we are."

Anna helped more around the house, and I helped also. I had learned how to mend clothing at school. Though we had little to eat, Anna kept up Momma's traditions. Momma was both there and not there. Anna became my new momma.

About six weeks after our move to Hongkew, Natasha is the next person I lose.

On my first day at the SJS she showed me around and introduced me to her friends. She helped me learn English more quickly. We did our homework together after school. At her house, we played with her toys and games. We were good friends ever since.

Though we were forced to live in Hongkew, I continue at SJS until the end of the school year. Once summer break begins, Natasha and I couldn't visit with each other. Stateless refugees are not allowed to leave Hongkew without a good reason. Somehow, I didn't think the authorities would give me permission to play with my best friend. I decide to wait until school started up.

Without Natasha, I feel so alone, but I still have Anna and Mary.

During the summer, Momma and Poppa decide the SJS was too far for me to travel to each day. I would begin the next school year at the Kadoorie School, which was closer. They never ask me where I want to go to school!

I argue with them. They don't change their minds. I'll never see Natasha again. That's how her name enters my list.

I never thought I'd add Anna's name to it as well. Anna's been with me my whole life. As soon as Anna told me that she'd be at the Kaplans' all the time until their baby was born, I knew she wouldn't be back. She said she would. She won't. People leave. They don't come back. As least Mary won't leave me.

ANNA AND ME TOGETHER

I WILL MISS ANNA. SHE AND I grew closer after Grandpoppa died, like she was trying to take his place. I think back to our good times together.

Each day before we returned home from school, we walked around. We sampled food from the various street stalls. I especially liked the sticky balls of rice in sesame seeds. Anna loved the roasted chestnuts so much I thought Shanghai would run out of them. Sometimes, we shared a baked sweet potato or sweet cakes.

As we ate, we shooed away flies and moved from the smoke.

Once, we bravely tried a noodle dish with soy sauce and what Anna called chile peppers. That and the tofu dipped in chili sauce were too spicy for us. "Ah!" I screamed after the first bite.

"It can't be that hot," Anna said before she tried it.

The man at the stall smiled at the face I made and gave us tea. Tea was the only drink we ever had at the stalls. We thought it was safe and weren't sure what was in other drinks.

I promised Anna I wouldn't tell Momma about our taste tests on the streets. We knew she would be furious about our eating street food. After all, Grandpoppa might have gotten typhoid this way.

We'd try different foods, and if we ate something not good for us, like fried dough, Anna would mimic Momma. "Don't ever eat that disgusting so-called 'food' they serve on the street. It's unsanitary, that's what is!" And we'd laugh. "I'll never let you out of the house unsupervised again!"

I couldn't picture my proper Momma venturing out on the streets to explore, let alone trying any of the food.

Anna took me to see *Pinocchio*. We lied to Momma about what we ate and where we went. "Do you think our noses will grow longer?" I asked quite seriously after we left the theater.

Figure 34: Food peddler

Figure 35: Food peddler

Figure 36: Street kitchen

Figure 37: Sweet potatoes

As Grandpoppa had done, Anna took me on adventures. We went into the Wing On and Sincere department stores across the street from each other on Nanking Road. Until the saleswomen chased us away, we'd try on hats and laugh at how we looked. We'd eye the fashions, knowing they were for the rich. We'd view the furniture and pretend we were helping our momma with ideas to decorate our lovely new apartment. We were always chased out.

At night, Anna "read" to me. She changed the stories, so I never grew tired of the few books I had. The three pigs became fifteen pigs who kept moving the walls and doors about. They argued whether to use sand, mud, or yarn to hold the houses together. The big bad wolf was the architect who blew their houses down because they had not followed his instructions.

Our fun lasted until Anna became too old to continue at SJS. Students attended until their fourteenth birthdays. After that, girls could take special homemaking classes. Anna said she learned more in those classes than the cooking classes we had in the lower grades. Boys would learn carpentry and how to fix radios. At fourteen, Anna did some odd jobs until she began helping the rabbi's wife. Slowly, she added more hours until she worked a full day.

Based on the news she had shared about the rebbetzin being bed-bound, she'll be at their house all the time. "The rebbetzin will need me even more," she said.

I need her, too.

I become aware of a strange feeling on my right hand and realize Ling has been tapping on it. Puzzled, I look at her. She gives me a piece of candy. It's a sour ball.

I'm no longer thinking about the past and my good times with Anna.

Figure 38: Wing On department store

Figure 39: Sincere Department Store

The jump rope is a bribe. Does she really think it will make me feel better? How can I be happy with so many people abandoning me?

Shortly, Momma comes out and asks if Anna has left. She says, "Too bad, we were going to work on wedding plans. She had something to give you. Did she?"

I hold up the jump rope. "Isn't she a dear? And soon there will be grandbabies."

Momma seems happier. Does she realize Mrs. Kaplan is planning the wedding and not her? Anna should have shared the same news with Momma that she shared with me.

I walk away toward Chusan Street and Little Vienna. I feel happy there, most of the time.

Momma Finds Her Way

"Wait!" Momma calls. "Show me where you get the hot water. When school starts, you'll leave early and might not have enough time to fetch any water."

Bewildered, I look at Momma. She's serious.

At the end of the lane, we turn the corner, and I point to the hot water shop. "The man there fills thermoses and containers from an enormous pot. I pay him with the bamboo sticks we keep next to the stove. There's a line in the morning, but it moves fast."

"Do we have enough bamboo sticks?"

"If not, I give him paper money that Poppa leaves and get bamboo sticks as change."

Momma should be teaching me. It shouldn't be the other way around. I hate doing Momma's jobs. I'm only eleven.

"That doesn't seem too difficult. I'll take care of the water tomorrow morning, but maybe you come with me the first time or two," Momma says.

Though Anna hasn't talked to Momma about wedding plans, I wonder what Anna told Momma during her short visit today. Did she tell her I could use help in the morning? Or is Momma just happy because Anna is getting married soon?

Adrienne Tropp

The next morning, Momma and I get the water together. *Together.* I like that word.

When we return, Poppa is gone. Momma notices a folded sheet of paper near his side of the bed. She opens it. "A map! Do you think he needs it?"

For a few minutes, Momma debates whether Poppa needs the map. When she raises her eyebrows slightly and nods at me, I know she's made a decision. "Hurry! Get this to him."

I race out but stop at the end of the lane since Momma can no longer see me. I look at the crumbled paper. It appears to be a marked-up map of Hongkew, written in English. I doubt Momma would know exactly what kind of map Poppa has. I can't read what I recognize is Poppa's tiny scrawl. *Why does he have this? Why does it seem to be in his handwriting?*

I have no idea where Poppa could be. I wander around; Momma will question me if I return too quickly. As usual, I marvel at the different shops on Chusan: bakeries, cafés, a kosher butcher, a German delicatessen, tailors, the lending bookstore, and the dry goods store. People call this area Little Vienna since it's so much like the European city, with its wide avenues and brick buildings. I look in windows, wishing I could buy something delicious. Few people can afford to buy, and therefore merchants have become creative. They sell a slice or two of sausage or cheese, part of a bottle of milk, or a spoonful of sugar.

Miraculously, I see Poppa, or someone who looks like Poppa, sitting at a table in a café. I enter. I hear English. My Poppa doesn't speak English. He and another man are focused on a slip of paper resting between their coffee cups. From what I can see, the paper is similar to the one I am holding. The man could be an English-speaking twin of Poppa's. I stand there a moment.

92

Pointing to the map, Poppa's twin says, "The radio must be moved immediately to—"

"Poppa?"

He and the other man look at me and take a deep breath. Poppa gets up quickly and nudges me toward the door. "Did you hear anything?" he asks me in German.

"No!" *What a strange question! Why didn't he ask what I am doing here?*

"Mr. Marcus needs my help moving a... a bed. We're planning the best route." He looks back quickly to Mr. Marcus.

Why is he telling me this—my poppa, who keeps things to himself? I clearly heard the word *radio*. Having a radio, which could transmit information from far away, is outlawed. Only Japanese news is allowed.

I realize Poppa is lying. His eyes dart about and his tone is angry. Does he wonder if I heard him speaking English? *I'm confused.*

I pull away from him and run out of the café. I see he's not following me and slow down.

"Did you find Poppa?" Momma asks when I come in the door.

"He was having coffee in Café Louis with a friend."

"Good, good," she says. "Was he happy to have the paper?"

"Yes." I don't tell Momma anything else. I wish I could talk to Anna about it, but I won't say anything to anyone, except Mary.

Summer and My New School

THE HOT, STEAMY SUMMER CONTINUES WITH nothing much to do. I think about how different last summer was. None of us would have imagined that the Japanese would issue a proclamation forcing us to move.

Most days, Ling and I play with the jump rope. Ling holds one end. I tie the other to a chair, the way Anna did. Waving my hands about, I try to get Ling to jump. As the rope comes around, it hits her shoulder. She backs away, her eyes watery. She couldn't be hurt.

Until she gets the timing right, she won't be able to jump rope. I stop for a moment and come up with an idea. Instead of jumping into a twirling rope someone else is holding, I could have her spin the rope herself and jump in.

I take it in small steps. First, Ling and I practice jumping up and down without the rope. We make silly sounds. I say, "Ribbit, ribbit," an English word I learned in school that is the sound frogs make. Ling says something like "Quack, quack!" Am I hearing correctly?

When she's comfortable jumping up and down, I bring out the rope. I demonstrate how to turn the rope and when to jump. She watches me for a while before she tries. She takes a small step toward the rope and stands still.

"Dummkopf." I hit my hand against my forehead. I adjust the rope, so the length is better for her. Now she succeeds at a few jumps. We both smile.

Ling and I teach each other to count—her in English, and me in Chinese. *Ee, ar, san, si, wu.* It is a hard language. Her voice rises and falls as she says different words. She tries not to laugh at me. In listening to her, I realize our laughs are similar. We point to an object, and each repeats the word in the other's language. Ling remembers words better than I do. As the heat of the day worsens, I go in and she disappears.

In the early evening, Momma and I set up the flowerpot. Anna's visit has made a difference because Momma and I cook dinner together. Momma, who has never cooked a meal, manages to heat up our food. What little we have doesn't taste good. I miss our amah.

Over time, I hear Momma speaking Yiddish with a few women in the lane who it turns out have come from Poland. They tell her about their difficult trip on the Trans-Siberian railroad across Russia and then on a boat from Japan. Momma repeats their stories to me. With each retelling, their journeys become more dangerous and the boat rides more treacherous. I begin to feel it was a miracle they arrived in Shanghai at all.

Momma enjoys trading tales of horror with them. I think someone is teaching her cooking tips because our food gets better. From Momma's translations, I learn there was no country called Poland until 1918.

Momma once told Anna and me that her mother and father had moved to Berlin from Lodz. Czar Alexander's assassination had been blamed on the Jews. Uprisings followed in Jewish areas occupied by Russia. Her parents had been very happy until they felt it was unsafe for them.

Though Momma had been born in Berlin, she felt an attachment to Lodz because of family stories.

Grandpoppa's family, who had lived in Lodz, also left in the early 1880s, when he was ten years old. He didn't talk much about his life there. He was upset that sixty years later he and his family had to flee yet again, this time from Germany, where they'd thought they'd be safe.

It's sad to hear the Polish refugees have had a difficult time, but for Momma's sake I'm glad they are in Shanghai. Momma leaves our room to talk with them. It's been good for her.

Poppa still stays out late. Many evenings he comes home in a not-so-bad mood. I walk by Café Louis, where I saw him, a few times, but he is never there.

Everyone who leaves the designated area must have a pass. The Japanese use Jewish men who go by the initials PAO to check passes as people enter and leave. I'll need a pass to attend the Kadoorie School, which was built before stateless people moved to Hongkew. It was not having a pass that kept me from visiting Natasha all summer. Passes for school are issued by Mr. Ghoya, a Japanese official. The yentas tell frightening accounts of what it's like to appear before him with a request. Of course, Momma feels she should tell me. "So you'll know what to expect," she says.

I learn the passes come in pink and blue—one is good for a day and the other for a month.

Early one morning a week before school starts, I line up before the Stateless Refugees Affairs Bureau. The line is long and slow. Everyone, including me, is dressed nicely. From inside the building, I hear someone yelling in English, but no one answers. I reach the door and a small, well-dressed Japanese man jumps up on the desk, reaches across it, and slaps the face of the person standing across from him. "Don't come back," he shouts.

The woman standing in front of me says, "That's Ghoya. Don't worry. He likes children. Tall people are another matter."

Did my tall poppa ever get a pass from him? Was he yelled at, too? I've never seen Poppa with a pass, and anyway, he probably wouldn't tell us if he had tried.

I move further into the room. Ghoya stops ranting and waves for me to come forward. I don't move. The person behind me gives a gentle nudge, and I take a step. Ghoya says, "Come here, little girl. There's no need to be afraid."

I gulp when I see his pockmarked face and realize that we're the same height. I'm barely five feet. His British English is flawless, unlike the English I hear from the refugees but like the English we are taught at school.

"I need a pass for sch... school," I stammer.

In a kind voice, he asks me what school I attend.

"The Shanghai Jewish Youth Association School,"

"Speak up, little girl. You mean Mr. Kadoorie's school?"

"Yes," I answer, a little louder.

He waves me over to another table to get my pass, which is blue. I won't have to face him until next September.

"Education is very important, little girl. Anyone else need a pass for Mr. Kadoorie's school? Come to the front of the line."

The pass only allows me to go to and from school. The route is clearly marked, as are the school hours. I have a half hour before school in which to get there, and an hour after school to return to Hongkew. I was hoping to use the pass to sneak off to see Natasha, but I can see I won't be able to.

Day one of school is awful.

On the lawn of the u-shaped building, kids hug former classmates. I don't recognize anyone from last year.

A girl comes up to me and says, "Hi! I'm Zosia. You new?"

Figure 40: Ghoya

Figure 41: Sign from Shanghai Ghetto

"Yes, I'm Rachel. I was at the Shanghai Jewish School last year."

"Hey, come here," Zosia motions to two other girls and tells them I was at SJS last year.

One of them says, "So why are you here? Most of *those* girls went back to SJS." They walk away before I answer.

I notice the school building has two wings. Between them is the kitchen where our food is prepared. Initially, I lose my way. Outdoors, we do calisthenics, play soccer, and attend gym classes.

I study the same subjects in the Kadoorie School as I did at SJS, including Hebrew and Jewish studies.

My English improves. Like Anna, I struggle with recitation and dictation. I do well in composition and grammar. I like math and the math teacher.

I don't pay attention to the Japanese lessons. Japanese is new for everyone, and not many of us like it. We study Chinese, as we did at SJS. Our Chinese teacher doesn't realize we cheat. When a student figures out what the teacher is saying, that student calls out the translation in German. We have no trouble translating from German to English. It is too difficult to translate Chinese to English. Thanks to our method, the Chinese teacher is full of praise for us, his "brilliant linguists."

On the first day, I sit by myself at lunch.

Well, mostly. Two little girls whom I recognize from SJS join me. It's not the same as sitting with Natasha and my friends. I miss them. *How is their school day going?* I wonder.

About a month after the school year starts, Zosia and her friends walk by the long table where I'm sitting. One of them

Figure 42: Boys playing softball

Figure 43: Girls' phys ed class

points and says in a loud whisper, "Ha! Look at her with her with those babies. Only kindergartners will sit with her."

Why are they so nasty to me? What have I done to them?

A second girl confronts me. "Isn't your best friend a three-year-old Chinese girl? You played with her all summer because no one else wants to be with you."

Ling is not three; she's at least—

Zosia mumbles something to her friends.

One turns toward me as she says, "Okay, we'll leave her alone."

After school, I drag myself home. I won't go back.

As usual, Ling waits for me. I ignore her and run inside, where Momma sits on a chair, examining her nails.

"Have you heard the latest? It's bad, really bad. I don't know what we'll do. Mrs. Mendel has news the Japanese are defeating the Americans. It's happening everywhere they battle. And worse, Germany conquers more of Europe. More bombings. More ships sunk. The war gets worse."

"Stop!" I want to yell to Momma.

After she's been outside listening to the yentas, her news is dreadful. It's good that she goes out, but she doesn't need to tell me everything she hears. I have my own problems.

Poppa, on the other hand, tells us both that the yentas are repeating the Japanese propaganda from the radio. "It's not the truth."

How would he know? I think back to what he said about moving radios the day I gave him the map. Does he have different news?

I hate this life. It's hard here. Food is scarce. Our home is a single room. The news is always bad. We're sick most of the time, often from our food. And worst of all, everyone at the Kadoorie School hates me.

After a few days of me ignoring her, Ling doesn't wait for me. She hates me now too. Is she another person who's left me?

Momma listens to everyone's bad luck stories and tells me about them. She doesn't care about mine. Anna hasn't come by in weeks. Not only that but Poppa is gone all the time.

In the French Concession, everything was better. Our family lived together. We had more food. Our apartment had two bedrooms. I had a best friend. Both apartments we lived in were better than anything in Hongkew.

I want to go back.

After thinking about it, I decide to leave. I picture Natasha running up and hugging me. I picture Natasha's mom working out a way for me to stay.

I plan my escape.

My Not-So-Good Escape

A WEEK LATER, ON TUESDAY, I BEGIN the long walk to SJS. As I start out, I see students who were there last year. One of them, who was in my class, calls, "Rachel, are you coming back to SJS with us?

She tells me, pointing to the group, that all of them still go. Each school day, a lorry picks them up and returns them to Hongkew. Ghoya gave them passes at the start of the school year.

The truck driver doesn't say anything when I jump into the open truck with the others.

My luck is changing already.

When the lorry arrives at SJS, they hop off and run to the yard. I stay behind, hoping to see Natasha.

A few minutes later, she and a few girls stroll onto the school grounds. I call to her. She looks in my direction.

"Rachel!" she shouts and races toward me, "You're here! It's so great to see you!"

We hug. The other girls join in. All of us talk at once, bouncing up and down in each other's arms. Natasha pauses. "Why did you come today? I have school."

They stop jumping and look at me. As I start to tell them about my plan, the bell rings. The girls leave, except for Natasha.

"Well? What do you think?"

"I don't know if it's such a good idea. Last time… I can't just now. I'll be late." She waves at me as she runs toward the entrance.

I was right; Natasha is lost to me.

I'm not wanted anywhere.

Tears stream down my face. I wipe them away as I walk the blocks to the tram. I ride the British tramway until I reach the French Concession. I cross the street to connect to a French trolley. The width of rails in each area is different. I have always hated switching between the two, and today it's even worse.

I see Japanese soldiers. People from countries who are enemies of Germany left in early December the year Hawaii was bombed. Just days before the bombings in Hawaii, many of us watched the American soldiers board ships and leave. We thought then that they would only be away for a short time, that they had maneuvers elsewhere. When we heard the news on December 8, we knew the Americans were gone permanently. On December 9, Japanese soldiers appeared everywhere in Shanghai, including the French Concession and the International Settlement, where they had not been before.

I wander around the neighborhood where we once lived. Our family was happy there. The Japanese ruined everything for us.

I buy noodles from a street vendor, glad that I took some money Poppa left for hot water and other things. The area has changed in the few months I've been gone. I notice few Europeans about, fewer vendors peddling their wares, and more shuttered stores. I drag my feet up and down the nearly empty streets. I have no interest in looking in the store windows at the beautiful items few refugees could afford. I feel worse than I thought possible. The place I loved and didn't want to leave now offers me nothing. I wonder whether to say hello to Natasha's mother. I decide not to. I don't belong here any longer. The French Concession is lost to me.

I return to Hongkew, taking the open truck back with the SJS students. I wonder what happens during monsoon season. Do they still ride in this open truck?

One girl who is a year older asks me about the Kadoorie School. She is thinking of transferring. Some of them are tired of the long ride to SJS.

The next day, I'm back at my school; it's better than doing nothing. No one seems to have noticed that I was away.

October rains cause flooding. Rotting, rancid rubbish drifts through the waters that are almost knee deep for me. School is closed. Rickshaw drivers still run about picking up the few passengers who are out. The weather is cooler.

November and December of 1943 are icy cold. I bundle up in layers and lay beneath my blankets at night. At least

Figure 44: Flood, 1941

the ever-present flies and mosquitos of summer are gone. Not as many rats seem to scamper about at this time of year. It's a relief to be rid of these pests.

NEW YEAR, NEW PROBLEMS

DECEMBER 31, 1943. A NEW YEAR is about to begin. People rejoice in the streets.

"What's there to celebrate?" I ask Poppa.

Poppa answers in German, "Not much. It's a new year, and people tend to hope for better when a new year comes."

I ask, "Will next year be better?"

He lowers his voice. "I am optimistic. The war is turning in favor of the Allies. Berlin has been bombed, and an American general called Eisenhower leads the European forces. The Japanese emperor has announced to his subjects that the war is going badly."

I look at Poppa. I don't understand much of what he's talking about. However, I have no doubt that he is involved in things he shouldn't be. If he thought he would make me feel better by telling me good news, he's done the opposite. Thanks to Momma's tales, I've heard about people, mostly men, who were taken to the Bridge Prison and never seen again. The prison is infested with mosquitos, flies, lice, and rats. Prisoners are beaten and starved. *Please don't let Poppa be doing anything wrong.*

This year has been miserable. We moved to this horrible place, I'm not in school with Natasha, Anna's left, the amount of food has dwindled, my stomach grumbles constantly, and I run to the honey pot often. Worst of all, no one at school likes me.

I don't know where the idea comes from, but I say to Poppa, "Let's make some new year's resolutions."

"What a great idea, Rachel. I'll work harder to undermine the—"

My mouth drops open.

"Don't worry, bubbeleh. I only mean I will pray harder for this war to end."

Poppa is lying. Whatever he's doing, he doesn't need to know I'm worried about him. As I worry less about Momma, I worry more about Poppa.

Trying to sound cheerful, I say, "Good idea, Poppa!"

Last Wednesday, on the last night of Hanukkah, Poppa gave me some coins, Hanukah gelt. At the time I was glad to get them. Now I wonder even more about where Poppa gets money.

To make Momma happier, I decide to share Poppa's news that the Allies are driving German forces back and the Japanese are struggling.

"Poppa lives in a dream world. Everything is rosy," she says. "He believes our tiny room is spacious and our food plentiful and delicious. He doesn't face facts and never has, or we wouldn't be living like this. We'd be in our beautiful apartment in Berlin, dressing in the latest fashions and eating at the best restaurants. I should never have come here."

I can't believe Momma's forgotten about what happened to Grandpoppa when the Gestapo arrested him and what else happened on that horrible November night five years ago. She's forgotten that Anna couldn't continue at school and the business had to be sold to a German. I've heard

Poppa tell Momma that after the war, we will return, and life will be better for everyone.

Momma seems to believe only what the yentas tell her about astonishing Japanese victories. I sort of do, too, but I hope Poppa's right. Only the defeat of the Germans and the Japanese will make our lives better. Why do people fight wars anyway? Don't they know how scared it makes the children?

"Momma, this will be a good year. Anna's getting married."

"Yes, yes, a wedding and, soon, grandbabies." Momma's blue eyes glow.

If I include talking to Momma, I make four resolutions for 1944. I hope they work better than my plan to run away.

Poppa's Secret

I MUST FIGURE OUT WHERE POPPA GOES.
The easiest way is to follow him and hope I don't get caught. I trail him as he leaves the house early one morning. He enters a café, where he joins other men. I can't hear their conversation. He meets the same men at different cafés. After three days, I give up.

A week later, he leaves later than usual, and again I trail him. He enters a lane house. Another man enters after him, and I wait. No one else appears. My hand trembles as I quietly open the door. Standing very still and trying not to make a sound, I listen. After a moment, I hear various men in heavily accented English speak in hushed voices. "May the good news about the war continue," a man says. "The receiver needs to be moved again." They murmur in agreement. The man says, "We're here to discuss the shipment. It should arrive on Friday. Our courier will deliver it as usual. Mr. Marcus I and Mr. Marcus II will be lookouts again."

"Yes," says a person who sounds like Poppa.

"Be careful. The Japanese have increased their patrols," says the first speaker.

I don't hear anything more. The men seem to have moved away from the door.

This is terrible. Poppa is breaking Japanese laws. He could be jailed. I must stop him.

I watch the door to the house until the men come out, and I call, "Mr. Weiser."

He turns and looks at me. He shoos the other men away and walks over to where I'm standing.

"I take it you're not here to give me a map I left at home."

"Stop, Poppa, stop whatever you're doing," I plead as I pull on his arm. "You'll go to jail."

He guides me down the street toward a café. Inside, he speaks to me in English for the first time. "These men don't know my real name; we all go by Marcus." He doesn't say anything more until our drinks arrive.

"I'll not lie to you; I'll tell you some things. Much is not for your ears. Do you understand?"

I nod. In a way, it's nice that Poppa trusts me, but do I want to hear about his doings? "Since arriving in Shanghai, Grandpoppa and I began gathering information against the Germans and now the Japanese as well. We sent it to our American contacts. With our import/export business, we could easily relay information to people outside Shanghai who were able to help refugees. That's all I'll tell you about what we did. After the Americans joined the war, it became almost impossible to continue as we had been doing. My efforts became more important, and we needed to go underground."

I'm not listening.

"Your English?" I stammer. "How... when did you learn it?"

"I knew some before we left Germany. I studied on the boat and more here. Your grandpoppa pretended that I needed to learn English. We thought Momma, Anna, and you would be safer if you didn't know about our contacts with Americans."

Poppa's been lying. And he taught Anna and me not to lie.

"Rachel, you must keep this secret from everyone, even Momma. I hate that you have yet another burden. You've been through too much for someone so young."

"And the other men you were with, Poppa?"

"I cannot tell you anything about them. Trust me. If anything happens to me, remember, I've been working to make it better for others who struggle here and those who fight against Hitler's forces. Try not to hate your Poppa too much. Do I have your word?"

Poppa hasn't told me anything specific. I've made good on my resolution to find out what Poppa has been up to, but I wish I didn't. I realize that Poppa probably does have a better idea of how the war is going than the yentas on the street. Maybe things are better than what the yentas report.

Finding out what Poppa's been doing was resolution number one. Now, it's time to work on resolutions two and three, which I can do at the same time. I feel confident that resolution two will turn out well.

Help for Me

AFTER SCHOOL, I WALK UP AND down the lane calling Ling's name. I don't know where she lives. I've never seen her go into any of the lane houses. She just appears and disappears.

Eighteen days into the new year, I begin work on my last resolution. I lick my lips as I enter a pastry store, thinking of what I'm about to buy.

At lunch, I search for Zosia and her friends. I see them in their usual places and sit in an empty seat next to them. Zosia says, "Hi." The others ignore me. They continue eating and gossiping.

After I eat the terrible lunch that's served to us, I untie a small package, ruffling the paper as much as possible. Zosia and her friends sneak a look at what I'm doing but turn away quickly as I uncover a slice of pastry.

"Ooh!" I say loudly.

Again, the girls' heads turn toward me and then away.

I feel hopeful.

They whisper to each other and nudge Zosia, who says, "What do you have there? It looks good."

"A slice of Linzer torte. Would you like a taste?"

"No. It's yours."

I insist, and soon she takes a bite.

"This is so good," she says to her friends as she finishes her tiny piece.

I took the chance that anything besides our small lunch servings of bread, watery stew, and tea would be a treat.

"Yum." I take another small bite. Then, as if I just thought of it, I offer each of the girls some.

At first, they shake their heads no. But it doesn't take long for each of them to give in. I see smiles cross their faces as they taste the torte. My plan is working.

They thank me and begin to ask about where I bought the slice. Soon we're talking about other things—school, our families, the weather, where we're from.

Poppa's Hanukkah gelt has been put to good use!

They invite me to jump rope with them after school.

I show them a rope game Anna taught me. The rope turners call out an action for the jumper to take. At first, it's easy, like "touch your shoe." Before long, the actions become almost impossible. One person yells for me to braid my hair—impossible because my hair, like most of theirs, is short. One of the smarter girls tries to trick us with difficult math problems. Another calls out for us to spell an English word or give a Hebrew word.

We're laughing so hard we hold our sides.

What a great day! It's the best I've had in Hongkew. As we leave school, we joke and laugh. We quiet ourselves as we sneak past the PAOs, who are supposed to check our passes. We know they know we are returning later than we are supposed to.

Momma doesn't hear me when I come in. I'm not even sure she realizes I'm later than usual.

A week or so later, Momma waits for me when I return late from school. "The best news I have to tell you."

"The war has ended?"

"No, no. Anna visited today. She has a wedding date: the twenty-sixth of Adar."

I calculate. Now it is February and the Jewish month of Shevat. The wedding is about a month away. That's seems soon.

She tells Poppa more that night. "The date was selected for good luck—a Tuesday and in the lucky month of Adar."

Momma's already fretting over details. I hope she won't be disappointed and that Anna leaves me out of all this wedding planning.

Anna comes by that Sunday while I'm outside, to share the news with me. She hugs and kisses me. "I'm sorry I haven't come by in a long time. Not only was the rebbetzin's pregnancy difficult, but so was her recovery. She had her third girl, so, fortunately, we didn't need to worry about a bris. I don't know that she would have had the energy to cook and entertain eight days after having the baby."

"A girl, how nice," I say. I couldn't care less. The baby will keep Anna busy and away from home.

"The rebbetzin is doing well, and I think planning a wedding has lifted her spirits. I'm so lucky. I hope someday, little sister, you too will be as happy. I've missed you."

She couldn't have any idea of how much I've missed her and wanted to talk with her about Poppa and about school.

"There are some items to settle on yet. For one, I want you to be my bridesmaid. It would make me happy for you to have a part in the ceremony, and it's an honor."

"No, I don't want to do anything."

"Then it's the perfect job because there's nothing for you to do."

"Anna, if it's a job, there is something to do."

"You only need to walk down the aisle ahead of me and move to the side when Schlomo and I say our vows."

Anna doesn't wait for an answer as she hurries inside to our room. I follow. Momma jumps up and runs to her. "We have so much to talk about. Where will the ceremony be? And what about a reception?"

"Momma, everything is being taken care of by the rebbetzin and me."

"What do you mean, the rebbetzin?" Momma raises her voice. "She's not your mother. I am."

"Momma, I wanted your help, but since I'm marrying a yeshiva student, we must follow specific rules, about which the rabbi's wife is more knowledgeable."

"Oh." Momma slouches down in the chair and puts her hands over her eyes, but then she brightens. "Your dress! I can help you with that."

"A dressmaker and I have been working on it. I am using another bride's dress, which belonged to yet another bride." She laughs. "My dress was once a set of curtains hanging in the home of a wealthy Englishman before he returned to England. Since I'm taller, we're adding fabric to the bottom from some lace pillowcases I found for sale on the street."

I suspect Momma will be complaining to everyone that her own daughter won't let her help plan the wedding. If Anna thinks I'll help Momma get over her disappointment, she's wrong. Anna better figure something out, or she'll find her own mother isn't at the wedding.

"It doesn't sound like you need anything," snaps Momma. "You've probably even found a new momma and poppa to take our part in the ceremony, a religious set who will know what to do. My own daughter doesn't want help from her momma, the mother who carried her for nine long months and cared for her when she was sick. To some stranger she turns."

"Momma, stop it!" Anna says.

This isn't going well. Anna shouldn't talk to Momma that way.

"Momma, be happy for me! I came here today because I want you and Poppa to help me pick out my bouquet. The bouquet I'll keep forever. The dress will be passed on to another bride and no one will especially remember the reception, except Schlomo and me."

"The bouquet? Yes, I kept mine until we came to Shanghai. You're right. Your momma should be there to help with that."

I'm amazed at how well Anna is handling Momma. I need to learn from her.

I glance over to Poppa, who smiles proudly at Anna.

"And there is more. I want us to shop together for the bridal cake."

"The cake, too? *Mammele*, I should never have doubted you." Momma says to Anna.

Zosia and her friends want to hear every detail. A wedding. They are excited. It is something to look forward to.

PART 5

NEW BEGINNINGS

THE WEDDING

THE DAY OF THE WEDDING ARRIVES. Momma, Poppa, and I dress in our best clothes, which were older garments that we transformed into nicer ones. Neighbors pitched in with velvet or lace material from beloved clothing they once wore. Once dressed, we walk to the rabbi's house.

Anna hugs and kisses us when we arrive. She wears a long, flowing white gown with a lace veil. At the bottom of her wedding gown are white lilies embroidered against the slightly darker lace. I wouldn't have noticed if Anna hadn't told us about how the dress had been mended to fit her.

"Come in before the other guests arrive. Schlomo and I are about to sign our ketubah. We were waiting for you."

"Ketubah?"

"A marriage contract."

"Huh? You need a contract?"

"It's Jewish tradition. It states the husband's obligations to his wife."

Weird, I think.

"Do you remember Yakov? He helped Schlomo and me when the family moved to Hongkew."

I don't say anything, but I haven't forgotten him. I have even walked by the yeshiva a few times hoping to see him. I never have.

Anna continues, "Well, anyway, he designed the ketubah. He did the calligraphy and the intricate work on the three borders. Notice how each one has a different design. He used the rabbi and his wife's ketubah as a model."

She points to a large sheet of paper. I see large golden Jewish stars in each corner. Centered on the sheet are about twenty-five lines of Hebrew script, which I guess is the contract. What amazes me is the detailed decoration around the edges; each of the three borders has a different design.

Yakov has spent many hours on the ketubah. He's talented.

I ask Anna about the blanks.

"That's where Schlomo and I sign, and that," she points to another space, "is for two nonfamily witnesses. Yakov will be one."

I point to a colorful paper I see partly hidden underneath the ketubah, and I pull it out. "What's this? It's in Chinese?"

"That's our state wedding certificate. We need it before our Jewish ceremony."

This paper, which I look at more closely, is decorated with flowers, including a lotus at the top surrounded by peacocks along the sides. It's funny to look at the Chinese written from right to left and in a column, but Anna's and Schlomo's names are written as they would be on a German or English document, left to right.

As the ceremony starts, I walk down the five-foot-long aisle and stand under the chuppah, the canopy under which Anna and Schlomo will say their wedding vows.

Anna follows, walking elegantly down the aisle to where Schlomo stands. Both have wide grins on their faces. After their vows, Schlomo stomps on a glass to shatter it. I don't know why it's part of the ceremony, but I've heard about it before.

Guests yell, "*Mazel tov*, Schlomo! *Mazel tov*, Anna!" and break into song.

Anna and Schlomo each sit on a chair, raised by the male guests. Men and women dance around them, continuing to shout their congratulations. When the chairs are lowered, the newlyweds disappear for a short time. On their return, males move to one side of the room with Schlomo, and females to the other, with Anna.

I stand next to Anna, not knowing what to do. I stare at her. Because she looks so happy, I know she loves Schlomo, even though I doubted it at first. A few people say to me, "Mazel tov on your sister's *simcha*." Otherwise, no one speaks to me.

Everyone seems happy. Why aren't I? Tears well up in my eyes. I can barely hold them back.

Various wedding cakes are cut and served. I hide a few slices in a napkin, trying not to scrunch them. I feel like a thief stealing a valuable ring. My friends at school will be happy to have a slice.

People eat and drink. Men dance with men. Women dance with women. People sing and rejoice, each group with its own songs. It feels like two teams competing at a soccer match on the field at the SJS.

I don't know the dances, and I know only a few words to the songs the women sing, so I just watch. Anna comes over and puts an arm around me. "Are you all right? Don't you want to dance?"

"No. I'll watch."

"Are you sure?"

I nod.

"Schlomo and I are so fortunate. I can't believe how generous everyone has been. And the rabbi and his wife have been so gracious. Isn't this all so wonderful?" Anna pauses. "Please, Rachel, when you leave, take some of this food for yourselves, and make sure you take some cake for your friends."

I feel more guilty.

For another five or ten minutes, I continue watching the wedding guests enjoy the festivities. Watching Anna dance and sing, I realize how much she has become a part of this more religious world.

This is Anna's life, not mine. I make my way to the door and leave.

Back home, I lie on Momma and Poppa's bed and cry. Anna's married now, and my life will never be like it was before we came to Shanghai, nor even when we lived in the French Concession. Tears fall from my face onto the pillows. I realize all the things I'm missing.

I fall asleep holding Mary. She'll never leave me.

Momma and Poppa wake me when they come in. "Rachel, why did you leave? It was such a beautiful wedding, wasn't it? Didn't Anna look beautiful? And everyone was so nice."

Momma and Poppa discuss the wedding. Well, actually, Momma does the talking.

Poppa looks at me. "Rachel, are you all right?"

"Yes, I'm just happy for Anna."

That evening Momma describes the wedding to the yentas who crowd around to hear the details. With each telling the wedding becomes more elaborate and the presents more impressive. In the first telling, I learn that some people gave Schlomo and Anna a few coins, not much. They also received a mattress, a jar of jam, some coffee, a blanket, and two pillows. The jam becomes a basket of fruit, pillows are fluffy enough to sink one's head in, and the blanket is made of the finest wool. The money has blossomed into a fortune.

"My Anna," Momma tells the yentas, "is so lucky to have received so many wonderful gifts."

"Yes, yes," the yentas agree. "Such a beautiful girl, so blessed."

At school, I tell Zosia, Matya, and Sasha about the wedding. I'm not as bad as Momma, but I make the wedding sound better than it was. I tell them the dress was made just for Anna by some famous Shanghai tailor. I tell them baskets of flowers covered the room though Poppa only bought two. I double the number of cakes and tell of nonexistent Polish dishes people brought for the wedding feast. I wonder if they believe me, but I want Anna's wedding to sound wonderful, even if it made me sad. They can dream, too. When I pull out the slices of cake, their eyes widen. The slices are crushed slightly, but I know how good they will still taste.

"How delicious! I haven't eaten anything like this in so long. I bet we'll get cakes like this every day in America," Matya says. She lives in one room with nine others, including her aunt and uncle and their children, but she dreams of cakes.

"Who cares about the cakes. I just want no bugs in my rice," says Sasha.

"I want to turn on the water tap and drink from it. No more hot water man!" shouts Zosia.

Matya and Sasha think big. They imagine the beautiful clothes they will wear, the fine restaurants they will dine in, and the bedrooms they will have that will be larger than the apartments in which they now live. "No more passes, no more Japanese to learn, no more bugs everywhere," they call out.

They laugh as they think about living in America, and I dream of returning to my life in Germany.

The month after the wedding passes quickly.

Anna visits, without Schlomo, who spends his time studying Torah.

"Why are you wearing a scarf over your beautiful hair? Aren't you hot?"

"As a married woman now, I cover it for modesty. Soon, I'll buy a wig. For now, any extra money goes toward food."

I thought she showed enough modesty when she began wearing longer skirts and long-sleeved blouses after she began working for the rebbetzin. I thought once the hot, steamy summer weather began, she'd dress more comfortably. She didn't.

Anna describes her visit to the mikvah before her wedding and on the seventh day after her menstrual cycle started. In school, I learned about the ritual baths and how a woman immerses herself fully to be considered pure. Being immersed in the mikvah sounds wonderful and reminds me of the days in the French Concession when we had a bathtub.

Anna seems happy with the rituals that are part of being a religious woman.

She whispers to me, "Do you remember Grandmomma's ring, with the little diamonds surrounding the ruby?"

"I thought it was a flower with tiny, shiny petals. She wore it all the time, and she'd let me wear it for dress up."

"Poppa smuggled it out of Germany. He and Momma gave it to me for a wedding present."

I look at her. The dark, straight hair she once loved to brush was hidden. She seemed heavier under her long-sleeved top and full skirt. She had Poppa and Grandpoppa's features, which I have always wished for. With the changes, she hardly seems like my old sister; that one is lost.

Her life is different from the one Momma, Poppa, and I live. It's different from the way many students at the Kadoorie School live, but not all of them. Some follow more religious practices, but more of us don't. Because they know each other from synagogue, they tend to spend time together.

Anna tells Momma and me about the Passover seder, which lasted until almost one a.m. It was held at the rabbi's house, with screaming children running about. In our family of three, Poppa spent a few minutes retelling the story of Moses and the exodus from Egypt. When he finished, he said, "We are required to tell the story, not have a seder, a big fancy meal. We've done what we needed."

"Good!" I thought. "Momma wouldn't have known how to cook anything much."

I remember last year, when Anna brought us matzah and described how yeshiva students had made it here in Shanghai, in the courtyard of the Beth Aharon synagogue. The matzah, we knew, was necessary for those celebrating the holiday in which Jews don't eat leavened bread, though many Jews don't follow the tradition. The funny picture I had in my head was of students carrying the matzah on long poles to bake in gigantic ovens. I pictured the matzah drooping further and further to the ground with each step until it swept the street, like the train of a wedding dress. Then these supposedly *purer* matzahs the yeshiva students had made couldn't be used. I don't remember exactly how Anna described the process anymore; I like my image better.

Anna says she will come again in a few weeks. Her visit, she reminds us, will be the one-year anniversary of when we were forced to move to Hongkew. It's been a hard year.

A lot has changed for the worse, but we try not to complain. Everyone is struggling. Complaining won't make my stomach feel better. Complaining won't provide more food when there's little to be had. Complaining won't get me out of Hongkew—not now.

More than anything, it's Poppa and his activities that I think about. Was I better off not knowing what he was doing? I can't unlearn what he told me. When I see a Japanese soldier near our house, I hold my breath until he passes.

Does Poppa have any idea how I feel?

Just before the school year ends, one of the girls at the SJS gives me a message from Natasha. She wants to meet me on the first day of summer vacation.

Because the PAOs, the refugee guards, see me so often, they don't ask for my pass. I'm not going far but am frightened that I will be questioned. I have no trouble. Natasha and I meet and talk about school, but otherwise we don't have much to say. I'm still hurt by the way she treated me when I ran away to see her. I hoped she wanted to apologize, but she doesn't. We part. I know I won't see her again.

WHAT'S TRUE? WHAT'S NOT?

T HE SUMMER IS HOT AND HUMID. Zosia, Matya, Sasha, and I walk around, looking into shop windows in Little Vienna and dreaming of a better world. We sit on ledges watching people go by. One day, another girl joins us. She watches her little sister every day and has wandered over to near where I live. We like throwing a ball to the three-year-old, who runs after it. Another time, we pool our money to share a slice of strudel. It's not apple, which is my favorite, but just having a bite is good.

Since I'm not in school during the summer, I hang around our lane. One day, I see Ling leaving the hot water shop and run after her. When I catch up, I say, "Ni hao."

"Heh-wo."

Neither of us knows much else in the other's language. I should have paid more attention to the Chinese we were taught at school. I've even forgotten the numbers she tried to teach me. I pantomime jumping rope. She nods. Early the next morning, she waits for me outside my building. We play for a while. When it becomes too hot, I go inside.

I'm glad Ling is no longer angry with me. Renewing our friendship is the last of the resolutions I made at the end of last year. Ling doesn't come back for the next few days, and I worry that maybe she is still angry at me.

Then she appears again a few days later. For the rest of the summer, she waits for me outside my house once or twice a week. On the days she's there, I bring out the jump rope. My day is happier when I see her. Playing with Ling again means I've kept all my resolutions, but I haven't gotten what I wish for most. Even a genie from a lamp wouldn't help make the leaders of the world get along.

In early June, Poppa tells me Allied armies have launched an invasion on the beaches of Normandy, France. Then he has news about the Allies retaking areas the Germans formerly held. "I am hearing good news. Jews in Shanghai should find their lives getting better. We should have more food, maybe new clothes, and a better apartment. Be patient, bubbeleh! You'll see."

Poppa makes me hope this horror may be over soon and we'll return to Berlin. Maybe someone rubbed a bottle and the genie appeared.

But Poppa's news always upsets me. I shake. His knowledge comes at a risk. *Please don't let him get caught!*

By the end of July, the yentas have new stories to tell. Death camps. Their stories sound too terrible to be true. I have no idea what they mean by "death camps," and Poppa says nothing about them. He tells only of Russian and Allied victories.

Despite what Poppa says, nothing improves, especially at night. Each evening, we still cover our one tiny window with a blanket. The Japanese check that no lights shine from any houses or stores. They shoot at windows if they see any light. Many windows are taped. Poppa says it's to keep the glass in place if the window is broken. Ours is too small to worry about.

The air-raid sirens become common, and I am taught that the first blast lasting almost two minutes gives me enough time to hide, usually, under something. Two minutes seem like an hour, but Poppa assures me it's only two minutes. Momma, Poppa, and I talk about places to hide depending on where we are when a signal goes off. After the all-clear (two short blasts) we agree to meet back at the apartment or as close to the lane as we can get.

Poppa thinks Hongkew is safe. The Japanese won't bomb us, and the Americans know we are here. How safe could we be since we hear warnings so frequently?

The yentas, the yentas, the yentas. They tell of impending horrors. Nazi officials in Shanghai. A Japanese plan to round up and force all Jews into camps. I've never heard anything so crazy. How could they possibly move so many to one place? Oops! Except they forced refugees to move to Hongkew. Maybe it's not impossible after all.

The yentas are scary. Their torn and patched clothing hangs from their thin bodies. Their eyes are sunken, and they have become less energetic. They no longer run up to us with the latest news. I wish they would just keep quiet. Except for the yentas in Hongkew, life is tolerable.

Momma, like most of the refugees, listens to the yentas and believes them. Momma shakes as she tells Poppa and me about their latest news. "How will so many of us escape?"

Poppa says, "Nazi officials have been in Shanghai for years, and what we're hearing is old news. The Japanese haven't listened to the Germans. The designated area was meant to appease the Germans somewhat."

Is Poppa, right? Or are the yentas? I don't know whom to believe. I want to believe Poppa because he's my poppa and because he's involved in something. Maybe he's lying, so I won't worry. The yentas have no need to protect anyone. At school it is the yentas' information that spreads. Always the yentas and never the news Poppa shares.

One day, Momma and Poppa have angry words about his predictions. It's impossible to ignore.

"Well, just *maybe* the Japanese will start listening to the Germans," Momma snorts, mocking him. "You sound like Mr. Prime Minister, with your assuring pronouncements. You don't know any more than the rest of us."

Momma pauses a moment after her outburst. Is she wondering how the yentas get their information? Or how Poppa does?

"Didn't we learn anything from living in Berlin? This time, we must be smart. We can't wait. We must find a way to get out of Shanghai, and soon."

"Shanghai!" Poppa laughs. "You can't even get a pass out of Hongkew."

The rumor about the Nazi officer continues, and Momma shares the information with me. Supposedly, the Japanese will put the Jews on boats and send them from Shanghai. Instead of providing an escape, the boats will be sunk in the middle of the harbor.

That news definitely is not possible. It doesn't make any sense to kill people in Shanghai just because they are Jews. Rounding up people to put in a camp is one thing. It took boatloads and boatloads to get us all to Shanghai. Thousands and thousands of Jews have come here in a few years. Poppa has told me there are perhaps eighteen thousand or more. That's unbelievable, too. Anyway, there aren't enough ships to take us away. The rumors are too crazy to be believable.

Poppa reassures Momma and me. "I'm hearing from some Japanese authorities who should know that placing Jews in Hongkew was as extreme as the Japanese were willing to go. The official isn't sure why the Japanese seem to be willing to anger the Germans and protect Jews."

None of this makes sense. If no one is trying to hurt us, who is causing the air-raid alarms to go off? It isn't the Americans. If it isn't the Japanese, and it isn't the Germans, who is it? Then I think Poppa's information must be wrong. Maybe there is another enemy out there.

Like me, my school friends walk away when the yentas approach us. I wish I had ear closers so I couldn't hear what they say. Their information can't be right. We students haven't done anything. We've barely begun our lives. Even Anna is just beginning hers. We try to enjoy the summer vacation despite the heat and humidity and rumors.

Zosia, Matya, Sasha, and I meet a few times a week. Sometimes it's just one or two of us and sometimes all four. Every so often another girl or two joins us. We jump rope, talk, and wander around. Matya has a board game we play called Shanghai Real Estate that can take hours. We throw dice and move around the board. When we arrive on "Go," we get two hundred dollars. If we land on the spot with Sikh

Figure 45: Shanghai Millionaire

policeman, our numbered piece is sent to jail. We can buy properties called The Bund, Broadway, Nanking Road, and Avenue Joffre.

It is a sad game to play because I remember our first apartment with Grandpoppa, near Avenue Joffre and the stores on Nanking. Back then, Shanghai was not as hard a place to be. We were all so sad to live there at the time, but now I wish we could go back.

ANOTHER SCHOOL YEAR

A s THE NEW SCHOOL YEAR BEGINS, I'm not afraid to get my pass. Mr. Ghoya does like children. He's come to the Kadoorie School a few times during the 1943-1944 school year. We've heard that he practices with the more advanced music students and compliments them on their playing.

At the Purim play, he booed the evil Haman. He cheered Esther's and Mordechai's names when they were mentioned. They are the heroes who saved Jews. Ghoya has two sides to him—one of them is for the children.

Just as I arrive at the Refugee Bureau, he tells all the children to come to the front of the line. We don't have to wait. Two of the girls who went to SJS last year ask for passes to the Kadoorie School.

The 1944-1945 school year begins. This year I have friends who hug me on the first day. Our lunch portions are smaller. Our clothes are shabbier, but I have friends.

On the street the yentas complain, "So little to eat. So little to eat."

School is school. Most days I stay afterward to play. Sometimes when I get home, Ling is waiting.

As 1944 ends, we all hope the Allies will win soon. They must! They simply must!

People celebrate the new year quietly. This year there are no celebrations. People gather in the street and talk quietly.

During the year people became hopeful, then disappointed, then hopeful again.

As usual, Poppa is gone all day and late into the night. As 1945 begins, he seems to be gone even more. He doesn't worry about our smaller food rations, and he doesn't bring home extra food any longer.

The yentas, as always, are full of news, sometimes good news of Allied victories, but mostly horrible news.

With the warmer weather, young people in Hongkew climb to rooftops to view the American B-29s dropping bombs. They report fires in the distance. Sometimes we feel a gentle rumbling, especially when we are at school. From the noise, the bombings seem closer each day.

My friends and I discuss what this could mean. Matya says, "It's obvious. The Americans are coming to save us."

I wish I had her way of looking at things.

We don't fear being bombed. The Americans know that thousands of Jews are living in Hongkew, and that's why they stay away.

At school, we talk of little more than the end of the war. We all practice our English, so we'll be ready to greet the American soldiers.

At the end of March, Poppa tells me about an Allied victory after a fierce battle at a place called Iwo Jima. He sounds almost cheerful. I wonder about dead Japanese. How many of them have families? I'm glad the Allies are winning, but what about children in Japan? They haven't done anything bad. Is their food also rationed?

The yentas continue with their news, their horrible news: death camps in Europe; clothing, jewelry, and shoes piled high at these sites. Their stories can't be true.

Poppa doesn't tell me anything about death camps. He continues to tell of Russian and Allied victories across France and Western Germany.

On April 12, we hear Franklin Roosevelt, the American president, is dead. Many of us cry. He was our hope for an end to the war.

Zosia says, "Without the president, how can America win the war?"

"The generals are the ones who plan the war. And America has a vice-president to take over. Don't you remember learning that, you schnook?" Matya says.

On April 30, we hear Hitler is dead. This is news the yentas spread. Poppa confirms it. For once, their information is identical. People cheer when they hear this good news. The war will certainly end now.

On May 8, there is victory in Europe. People sing and dance in the streets. We quiet down when Japanese soldiers are near.

"Be careful," Poppa says. "The Japanese still control Shanghai. They must know about their losses in the Pacific. There's no telling how they may react."

"Poppa," I promise, "I won't do or say anything when they are near."

"No, not just when you see them. You must be watchful all the time."

HONGKEW IS BOMBED

SUMMER VACATION COMES AGAIN—ANOTHER HOT, HUMID, boring summer.

Shortly after we're out of school for the summer, Poppa tells me of another Japanese defeat at the hands of the Allies at a place called Okinawa in the Pacific.

On July 10, Tokyo is attacked. Both the yentas and Poppa report that the capital of Japan has been bombed. I don't mind listening to the yentas now. They have news before Poppa returns to our room at night. And they report the same news.

On July 15, there are bombings near Hongkew. From late morning until midnight, most of us in Hongkew hear bombs exploding along the Whangpoo River. Shrapnel comes down. The yentas chant, "The Americans are here! The Americans are here!"

That's good! The war must be about over at last.

Along with my friends, I rejoice. "No more Hongkew. No more Shanghai. No more rations. America, here we come!"

I picture The Bund packed with people and boats lined up to take us away.

On Tuesday, July 17, bombs explode in Hongkew. The day begins just as any other during the summer. I play outside with Ling and go inside as usual to avoid the heat. Just after noon, I hear planes in the distance. They get louder and louder. Air-raid sirens go off.

Momma and I dive under a mattress, as we have practiced. We hear objects crashing. Our apartment shakes, but luckily neither the ceiling nor the walls cave in.

When the all-clear signal sounds, we check our room for any damage. Everything seems fine, except for a few objects that have fallen from the tabletop. Even our small, taped window remains in one piece. We run to the street.

Momma calls "Rachel, stay close! Don't wander off!"

People scream, "I've been hit!"

Others call out, "SACRA's been hit." SACRA is where Matya lives.

Poppa comes racing down the lane. "You and Momma okay?"

I nod, unable to speak.

"Good! Many have not been so fortunate," Poppa says. "The Americans hit the radio station. Rumors are flying. It will be hours before we learn the extent of the damage."

People rush about. As I run toward SACRA, I realize people are running the other way.

"The jail! The jail! There's help there!" people shout.

Flames are seen near SACRA. Smoke fills the air. Fire engines zoom down streets.

The wounded hold their hands to their heads. A mother clasps a bloody child as she runs toward the jail. A man with one leg hobbles toward help.

A child cries, "Momma! Momma!"

An elderly man calls for someone, maybe his wife.

Everywhere the wounded run about. *How can they all possibly be helped?*

The blood is sickening. I swallow hard. I see others, both Chinese and refugees, turn ghost-like.

Inside the gates of the Ward Road Jail, in an open area, a temporary place is set up in which to operate. First-aid trucks, the Chinese, and refugees rush to the prison yard carrying the injured.

Refugee and Chinese doctors stand opposite one another, yelling. No one on either side understands the other until a Chinese doctor steps forward. He translates, "Give the western doctors what they need to operate with."

The quarrel ends and western doctors have what they need.

The doctors quickly examine patients. Some are moved closer, and others farther away from where the doctors work. Are they deciding whom to treat first?

One person who is moved farther away screams, "Help me! Help me! I'm bleeding! I don't want to die!"

Another cries, "Me first!"

A third says, "Here! My family…" and his voice trails off, but he is in the queue for the doctors.

I close my ears. I can't listen anymore. I'd hate not to have been chosen. To have no hope of treatment seems horrible.

The earliest arrivals get shots, which calm them down, and their wounds are treated. Soon supplies are gone and people begin tearing up sheets and their clothing to use as bandages. I help tear up scraps. Women prepare tea for the wounded. Blankets and pillows appear, on which the wounded are placed. Chinese and Jews work together to help them. I spot Ling near the end of one of the lines. She moves toward me and helps pile up the scraps.

As the sun sets, the wounded seem to have all been treated, even those in the group that had been moved farther away.

The Chinese doctors stand around, doing little. A bystander tells me Chinese doctors require payment before they help anyone. It is their way. Some who had money offered too little.

I don't understand how trained doctors can just stand there. Wounded Chinese turn to our doctors. They offer money and are upset when it isn't accepted. That is not our way.

Back at our room, I try not to think of what I have seen, but I keep seeing blood oozing from faces, arms, legs, and underneath tattered bits of cloth. Of course, before today, I knew people were hurt and killed in war, but today I saw how terrible it is. Innocent people. How could anyone not hate war?

From the news I hear, the fires around the city are all out. Children pitched in to help the bucket brigade while I was busy at the jail.

"Mary," I say, "you're lucky no bomb can harm you. You'll never scream out in pain." I hold her tightly as I fall asleep.

Later, I learn that kindergarteners at SACRA were evacuated before the bombings.

Unbelievably, the Chinese bring food and money to refugees. Momma says it is their thanks for helping them. *They have so little*, I think, *and yet they are sharing with us.*

Jews and the Chinese alike mourn their dead. They are not so different from us.

I visit Matya. Her head is bandaged, and her right hand is covered in gauze from burns. She cries, "How could the Americans do this? How can anyone do such a thing?"

I don't answer.

"I won't go to America! I couldn't live with the people who did this to me. Why me? I haven't done anything to them."

I am thinking the same thing. Maybe when Matya is better, she will feel differently. I hope so. She had wanted to go to America before the bombing. She had talked about it perhaps more than anyone else I know.

Rumors fly. The one I hear most is that the Americans bombed the area by mistake. I could never tell Matya that.

Poppa disagrees. "They had no choice. The Japanese radio station had to be destroyed."

Ling and I get together most days, but she's not interested in playing and doesn't say much. I hope none of her family was hurt or killed in the bombing, but I don't have the words to ask her. One day, she shows me a book and points at it and then at herself.

At first, I think the book is about her, but when I look at it, I realize it's in English.

I puzzle over what she wants.

She watches me and realizes I'm confused. She points to her eyes and the book. I catch on. She wants to learn to read.

The Swiss Family Robinson, which she holds, is too hard. I wonder how she got it.

I think about how I learned to read. I use *The Swiss Family Robinson* to show her how the different letters look, and we work on sounds. She learns quickly, and I decide to teach her some words.

I draw pictures. She laughs at them. My cat doesn't look like a cat but rather a whiskered face on a strange building. Unfortunately, we don't have much use for the words *cat, bat,* or *sat;* I remember starting with *-at* words.

Soon after the bombing, Anna visits to see how we're doing. I tell her about the difficulty I am having teaching Ling. She returns two days later with a few books. They are picture books—one in Hebrew and the other English. I laugh as I picture Ling speaking Hebrew to everyone's surprise. The books are perfect!

Ling learns quickly, even remembering words I taught her a while back. It's not long before she reads a few simple words and speaks a few short sentences. Her L-sound never comes out right. She says "heh-wo" for hello and "wook" for look.

I don't laugh, though her speech sounds funny. I sound even funnier speaking the Chinese words we were taught at school.

The air-raid signals continue for weeks, but no bombs fall on Hongkew.

In early August, I hear about a bomb, the worst ever made. Poppa tells me that the Americans have unleashed this bomb over a Japanese city. And three days later, he tells me the same thing has happened in another Japanese city. News of the horrible deaths these bombs caused begins to reach Hongkew. What I hear can't be true.

"It can't be long now," he says.

The yentas tell anyone who will listen, "Bombs in Japan. Big bombs. The biggest ever."

I shudder, remembering how bad the bombing was in Hongkew just a few weeks earlier. *Doesn't anyone remember? Does anyone care about the dead and wounded? How many innocent Japanese children have been hurt, like Matya? Poor children.*

Eight days later, the yentas are on the street yelling, "The war is over! It's over!" They scream out other words, bad words about the Japanese.

Poppa comes home with the same wonderful news. "The Japanese have surrendered. The war is over."

People dance and sing in the streets. No one is afraid of Japanese soldiers anymore. They seem to have disappeared. We remain cautious.

I see Ling in the street. She claps and says, "Over. Over. Good, no?"

"Yes, very good."

She too jumps up and down, and one of the Jewish women grabs her hand and she joins the dancing. This is the happiest people have been since we arrived in Shanghai.

"Wait!" I say and run up to our room. "Mary," I yell, "it's over. The fighting is over." I hug her tightly and run out clinging her to me.

"Here!" I say to Ling as I return.

Ling shakes her head.

"Yes! Her name is Mary. I want you to have her."

She points to herself and says "Mary? Me?"

I point to her and say, "Ling," and then I point at Mary and repeat her name.

She looks closely at Mary and then at me. "You?"

"She looks like me, yes!"

"Doh je!"

I look at Ling holding Mary and regret giving her my doll.

Figure 46: On The Bund to celebrate victory, 1945

People stay up into the early morning hours celebrating. And I spend my time picturing our family returning to Berlin.

When Anna visits, we celebrate the American victory and catch up on news.

I tell her I gave my doll to Ling, still feeling sad about it.

"What a wonderful thing to do! You realize this is probably the first toy she's ever had. Most Chinese children don't have toys, and certainly not a doll as beautiful as Mary. And best of all, when she looks at Mary, she'll remember you."

Anna's right, and I don't feel as sad about giving her to Ling. I can have lots of other Marys if I want, and it will be her only one.

The 1945-1946 school year begins. We don't stand in line to get a pass from Ghoya. At school, we celebrate our new freedom. We leave the school grounds and walk around the city. No Japanese soldiers appear. No PAOs stop us.

With the Allied victory come American soldiers, jeeps, food, and jobs. It is a joyous time. We have more to eat, more medicine for the sick, more people working for good wages. The Americans don't seem so bad. They place children on their jeeps and take pictures and give us candy.

Slowly, though, we all learn about what happened in Eastern Europe—gas chambers and the deaths of millions of Jews. No longer are we so joyous. People line up to search the list of survivors that is posted daily.

We are thankful for our lives, and Hongkew doesn't seem horrible now; we are alive. Momma says, "How smart your poppa was to get us out of Germany."

My family and I realize we will never return to Germany after that country murdered so many in the camps—so many innocent people who suffered because they were Jewish.

My friends and I wait for visas so we can go to the United States.

Afterword

R ACHEL WEISER DIDN'T EXIST, AND NEITHER did
  her family.

The historical events in her story did happen. About
twenty-thousand Jews found their way to Shanghai from the
mid-1930s until the United States entered the war in 1941.

The proclamation with which this story begins was issued
on February 18, 1943. It forced refugees who arrived in
Shanghai after 1937 to move to a one-mile area in Hongkew,
a section of Shanghai. Rachel's family had to move.

The Americans bombed Hongkew on July 17, 1945. About
two hundred Chinese and forty Jews died in the bombings.
Chinese and Jews worked together to help the wounded.

Jews who had migrated earlier (before the 1930s) helped
the newer refugees until the number became too large for
authorities to provide them with adequate food and shelter.

At one point, before December 1941, Jewish immigration
to Shanghai became restricted. The community that was
there already couldn't support any more refugees.

In 1940, six thousand Jews in Lithuania were able to
escape. Without permission from his superiors, a Japanese
official issued visas for families to emigrate to Japan. They
lived there until November 1941, when the government

moved them to Japanese-controlled Shanghai, the only safe place for them.

Of those who arrived in Shanghai, many had little or no money, no food, no work, and no place to live. One meal a day was normal, and it was often obtained from a soup kitchen.

Rachel and her family were better off than most who lived in Shanghai. She had a nicer home and enough food, at least when her family first arrived. Most refugees lived in rooms as small as two hundred square feet, often with three to ten people. Others even less fortunate were crowded into Heimes, homes established to house them, where they had only one bed.

Jewish refugees in Shanghai recreated some of their European culture. Newspapers, theaters, orchestras, schools, nightclubs, recreational opportunities, sport competitions, European-style restaurants, and coffeehouses were established.

Though these immigrants tried to make themselves as comfortable as possible, their lives were difficult.

Some people I contacted had such terrible recollections of their time there—so much so that they would not allow me to interview them.

In the story that you've just read, I have taken some liberties with events. One involves what took place on July 17. Rachel is home, but it is unclear whether school was in session. Doris Fogel remembers hiding under the desk as the bombings began and not reuniting with her mother for, as she says, "a period of time." Lilly Toufar and her mother were eating lunch as the bombs fell. For the purposes of this story, Rachel needed to be home.

The Kadoorie School was outside the area designated for Jews. It is not clear whether children needed passes from

Ghoya, the cruel Japanese official responsible for handing them out. Since Ghoya's cruelty angered so many of the refugees, he needed a scene in the story.

World War I was called the "war to end all wars." It was far from that. Since its end in 1917, more than two hundred twenty-five wars have been fought. How many have died or were severely wounded since that war ended? How many became homeless or were left starving during and after these wars? Rachel and her family were fortunate compared to them.

Genocide—the destruction of a people because of their race, religion, ethnicity, or national origin—continues to this day. According to the website *Journey Through the Holocaust*, fifty-five million lives have been lost in eighty-nine genocides since World War II ended.

As *Shanghai Losses* was being prepared for publication, another war, many are calling a holocaust, is being fought in Ukraine.

The term *holocaust* (or genocide) became more familiar after WWII. But the worst recorded genocide occurred in the Americas well before then. It's been estimated that between 1400 and 1924, more than fifty million Native Americans were killed.

The next-largest recorded genocide is of the eleven million people whom the Nazis killed. More than six million were Jews. Romas (gypsies), homosexuals, Jehovah's Witnesses, Germans with disabilities, and Communists number another five million. Again, Rachel and her family were among the more fortunate. They escaped to Shanghai.

Hatred of those who practice Judaism is called anti-Semitism. It continues to this day, even after Hitler's horrendous attempt to murder Jews.

I hope you will see Rachel's story on a larger scale. So many suffer because of their races, religions, ethnicities, or nationalities. May we not forget, and may the future be better for them.

Figure 47: Shanghai Jewish Refugees Museum

Timeline of Events
Related to Story

Mid-1800s Baghdadi Jews from the trading center of Baghdad in Iraq arrive in Shanghai and become wealthy business leaders.

1881-1884 The period in which Rachel's grandparents leave Lodz during uprisings against Jews after Tsar Alexander II's assassination. Lodz, located in the Pale of Settlement—a large area created for Jews by Catherine the Great in 1791 in southwestern Russia—is now part of Poland.

1904-1905 Jews, escaping Russian pogroms (attacks on Jews), emigrate to Shanghai.

1917 In February, revolutionaries in Russia overthrow the tsar. In October, the communists gain power. White Russians (supporters of the tsar) and Jews flee the country. A great many find their way to Shanghai.

July 19, 1932 Rachel is born in Berlin, Germany.

August 1937 Battle of Shanghai is fought. Japan gains control of much of Shanghai, except for the French Concession and International Settlement.

November 9, 1938 Night of the Broken Glass, originally called the November Pogrom (now known as Kristallnacht), is the night when Jewish businesses and synagogues in Germany are destroyed. Rachel's grandfather and many Jews are arrested.

December 1938   Anna and Rachel's grandfather leaves for Shanghai.

March 1939   Rachel and her family leave for Shanghai on a six-week ocean voyage on the *S.S. Conte Rosso*.

September 3, 1939 War begins in Europe.

December 7, 1941 Japan bombs Pearl Harbor, a US naval base in Hawaii. America enters the war. In Shanghai, people hear the news on December 8. Foreigners from Allied nations flee Hongkew since they are no longer safe.

February 18, 1943 Proclamation is issued for refugees to move to Hongkew.

May 18, 1943   On this day, the proclamation goes into effect. Passes are issued to people who can prove they have legitimate reasons to leave Hongkew.

June 6, 1944   Called D-Day, this is the day when Allied forces invade Normandy, France. The Allies begin to retake land the Nazis hold from previous victories.

July 1944   Russian forces discover an abandoned Nazi death camp, verifying rumors of their existence.

April 1945	President Roosevelt dies on April 12. Hitler, seeing the imminent end of war, dies by suicide.
May 8, 1945	VE-Day, when victory in Europe is declared. German forces surrender to the Allies.
July 17, 1945	American bombs fall on Hongkew.
August 6, 1945	Atom bomb is dropped on Hiroshima, Japan, causing much death and destruction.
August 9, 1945	Another atomic bomb is dropped, this time on Nagasaki, Japan.
September 2, 1945	World War II officially ends.
1946-1948	Jews leave China as the communists take power. Most emigrate to Australia, Canada, Israel (then known as Palestine), and the United States. Some return to their homelands.

LEARN MORE

Allies: During World War II, the United Kingdom, the Soviet Union, the United States, and China had joined forces to defeat the Axis powers.

Axis powers: Among the countries who fought on the Axis side were Nazi Germany, the Kingdom of Italy, and the Empire of Japan.

Baghdadi Jews: Jews from Baghdad, Iraq, found their way to Shanghai in the mid-1800s after living in India for a time. This wealthy group held British citizenship, which meant they were unable to stay in Shanghai after Japan joined the Axis Powers (which consisted primarily of Germany and Italy) against the Allies (including the British and Americans). The Baghdadis earned their fortunes from trade, including opium. Among these families were the Sassoons and Kadoories, who assisted the poorer Jewish refugees after their arrival in the 1930s.

Chinue Sugihara: Sugihara was a Japanese diplomat who saved the lives of thousands of Jews. Rachel and her family wouldn't have known his name, and it's doubtful that many of those he saved would have recognized his name either. When he was assigned to the Japanese embassy in Lithuania, he provided between twenty-two hundred and six thousand visas for Polish Jews to escape. He had never received official permission to issue these visas. For various reasons, he was unable to provide visas to Lithuanians. He and his wife hand wrote most of them to enable Jews to flee to Kobe, Japan.

Sugihara is honored as one of the Righteous Among the Nations (see below).

Feng-Shan Ho: From 1938 to 1939, this man issued large numbers (perhaps thousands) of visas for those who wanted to leave Vienna. It's possible that any Austrians who traveled on the *SS Conte Rosso* along with Rachel's family obtained their papers from Feng-Shan Ho. He is remembered as one of the Righteous Among the Nations (see below).

Ghoya, Kano: Ghoya was the Japanese official put in charge of the ghetto. He was the official who gave out permits for people to leave the ghetto. He was a small man who spoke excellent English.

Horace Kadoorie: The wealthy Kadoorie family funded places of worship and schools for Jewish immigrants in Shanghai. The Shanghai Jewish Youth Association, or SJYA school was better known as the Kadoorie School. Horace Kadoorie realized how important education was to these children and set high standards for the school.

Kadoorie School: The seventeen teachers at this modern SJYA (Shanghai Jewish Youth Association) school educated roughly six hundred children in kindergarten through ninth grade. The school followed a British curriculum, with instruction in Hebrew, Jewish worship, English, French, arithmetic, history, music, and gymnastics. During English classes, students practiced writing and speaking. Girls were introduced to cooking classes and were taught manners. The forty-five-minute classes were held from eight o'clock a.m. until one p.m. Activities were offered after school. For those over the age of fourteen, trade classes were held for boys and secretarial and cooking classes were offered to girls.

Laura Margolis: In the novel, she is referred to as an "American lady" who aided the refugees. Sent to Shanghai by the American Joint Distribution Committee, she arrived in May 1941. Once there, she updated the soup kitchens that provided one meal a day to more than eight thousand refugees. After the Japanese attacked Pearl Harbor, Margolis became an enemy alien and interned in a camp for about seven months before she was released as part of an exchange.

Leo Meyer: Horace Kadoorie recruited Leo Meyer as his school's physical education teacher. Meyer's name was recognized by many in Shanghai because of his soccer skills. He taught and coached boys in soccer. Classes were held on the lawn between the two wings of the school.

Lucie Hartwich: She emigrated from Berlin and became the headmaster and a teacher at the Kadoorie School (or SJYA school). Horace Kadoorie met her on board a ship heading to Shanghai. He was impressed with the English classes she held while on the ship and offered her the position of headmistress at his school. Students remember Hartwich as someone who pushed them to learn English, since most students would eventually emigrate to English-speaking countries.

Mirrer, or Mir Yeshiva: The Mir Yeshiva was among the most prestigious schools for Jewish learning in Europe. Originally from Poland, all its students and teachers received visas from Sugihara. They journeyed on the Trans-Siberian railroad to Vladivostok, in southeastern Russia. From there, they sailed to Japan and were welcomed in Kobe. As Japanese forces planned to attack Pearl Harbor, the yeshiva students were sent to Shanghai.

Pearl Harbor: The Japanese navy bombed Pearl Harbor on the island of Oahu in Hawaii on December 7, 1941 (December 8 in Shanghai). After this American territory was attacked, the United States joined the Allies in the war against Japan and Germany.

Righteous Among the Nations: An honor given to non-Jews who risked their lives during the Holocaust to save Jews. Their 27,921 names from 51 countries are etched on the Wall of Honor in Jerusalem.

Russians: Many Russians left Russia in the early 1900s to avoid pogroms, which were violent attacks on Jews, and because Communist Joseph Stalin had become its leader.

Jacob Schiff: Although Schiff died in 1920, scholars believe his large loan to the Japanese during the Russo-Japanese War (1904-1905) may have influenced the Japanese to take a kinder approach toward Jews during WWII than the Germans would have liked.

Shanghai: In the late 1930s, Shanghai had a population of nearly three million and was among the largest cities in the world. Located on Asia's longest river, the Yangtze, and near the South China Sea, it also has one of the world's largest ports. The city had been divided into the French Concession in 1849 and the International Settlement in 1863. British and American citizens lived in the International Settlement until the bombing of Pearl Harbor. It was a city of great wealth and great poverty.

Sino-Japanese War: A war involving Japanese forces against the Chinese. In 1937, the Japanese bombed Shanghai and quickly gained control over most of the city, except for the French Concession and International Settlement. Since neither the Chinese nor the Japanese chose to issue visas, none were required until August 1939 (several months after Rachel and her family arrived). Therefore, thousands of Jews found their way to the port city of Shanghai. The Japanese gained control of the entire city after December 1941.

For Further Reading

Books About the Holocaust

Abramson, Ann. *Who Was Anne Frank?* New York, Penguin Workshop, 2007.

The story of Anne Frank's life, starting before she and her family went into hiding and spanning the period during and after they lived in the Annex. For ages 8-12. *Anne Frank: The Diary of a Young Girl* may be better suited to teens.

Coerr, Eleanor. *Sadako and the Thousand Paper Cranes*. New York, Puffin Books, 1977.

A story about a young girl who died of radiation from the bomb dropped on Hiroshima in 1945, which is what brought about the end of WWII. For ages 6-10.

Gratz, Alan. *Prisoner B-3087*. Scholastic, 2013.

A true story for ages 10-14 about a boy from Poland who endured life in ten concentration camps.

Herman, Gail. *What Was the Holocaust?* Penguin Workshop, NY, 2018.

A good introduction to the Holocaust, with illustrations by Jerry Hoare.

Hopkinson, Deborah. *We Had to Be Brave: Escaping the Nazis on the Kindertransport*. New York, Scholastic Focus, 2020.

This book for ages 8-12 shares the story of the 10,000 children who were sent to Great Britain from 1938-1940 to escape the Nazis.

Lowry, Lois. *Number the Stars*. Clarion Book, 2011.

Historical fiction about how the Danish Resistance smuggled almost 7,000 Jews from Denmark into Sweden. The story follows a ten-year-old through the ordeal. For ages 10-12.

Preus, Margi. *Village of Scoundrels*. Harry N. Abrams, 2020.

Readers ages 10-14 will learn about a French village that saved thousands of Jews. The teenagers in the town had been chosen to attend the special school there and put their talents to use.

Yolen, Jane. *The Devil's Arithmetic*. Penguin Young Readers Group, 2004.

A 12-year old Jewish girl is mysteriously transported back to the time of the Nazis. As her story unfolds, she is arrested and sent to a concentration camp. The book realistically shows what it was like for prisoners. It is recommended for ages 10-12, though it may be better for more mature readers.

Books About Children Who Became Refugees

Adewumi, Tanitoluwa. *My Name is Tani...and I Believe in Miracles (Young Readers Edition): The Amazing True Story of One Boy's Journey from Refugee to Chess Champion*. Thomas Nelson, 2020.

Adewumi's family fled the terrorist group Boko Haram, which was imposing terror on many in Nigeria. In the United States, Adewumi took up chess and became the New

York State champion. His autobiography is for ages 8-12.

Gratz, Alan. *Refugee.* Scholastic Press, 2017.

Three stories of refugee children—two boys and one girl, from Nazi Germany, Cuba, and Syria. Though from different time periods, the children share some common problems and escapes on water. For ages 9-12.

Hiranandani, Veera. *The Night Diary.* Puffin Books, 2018.

This story is about a half-Muslim, half-Hindu girl who must travel back to India across the partition that separates India from Pakistan. For ages 8-12.

Ho, Minfong. *The Clay Marble.* Square Fish, 1993.

Twelve-year-old Dara escapes from her war-torn village in Cambodia with her mother and brother. She becomes separated from them and finds a way to take care of herself. For ages 10-14.

Lai, Thanhhà. *Inside Out and Back Again.* Harper Collins, 2013.

Ha and her family flee from Saigon as the Vietnam War ends, finally settling in Alabama. Written in verse, for ages 9-12.

Park, Linda Sue. *A Long Walk to Water: Based on a True Story.* Clarion Books, 2010.

The story is about two 11-year-old Sudanese children whose lives intersect. Salva is one of the lost boys of Sudan, the approximately twenty thousand refugees who walk the continent of Africa searching for their families, and Nya, who spends hours each day walking to fetch water. For ages 10-12.

Rouse, Victorya. *Finding Refuge: Real-Life Immigration Stories from Young People.* Zest Books, 2021.

Rouse introduces readers 11 and up to 30 stories told by the refugee children who came to America from around the world. Included are backgrounds on their countries, as well as their motivations for fleeing their homelands.

Trebincevic, Kenan and Susan Shapiro. *World in Between: Based on a True Refugee Story.* Harper Collins, 2021.

Eleven-year-old Kenan, a Muslim living in Bosnia, loves soccer. Because of the war between Muslims and other religious people, Kenan and his family are stuck in their house for ten months with little to eat, surrounded by fighting, until they are able to leave with the help of others. For ages 8-12.

ACKNOWLEDGEMENTS

Writing itself is solitary. But the gathering of material involves the help of many. Once I committed to telling a story about Jews in Shanghai, many sources emerged.

Among the first was Judy Schumer, a friend who was born in Shanghai. She loaned me the documentary *Shanghai Ghetto* and several books, including *Strange Haven* by Sigmond Tobias, who told of his experience there.

On a trip to Shanghai in 2010, I saw Hongkew and an exhibit on the Jews of Shanghai at the former Ohel Synagogue.

Later, I was able to see parts of the exhibit at the Jewish Museum in Baltimore and at the Chinese American Museum in Washington, DC. As I write this, an exhibit has just opened at the Illinois Jewish Holocaust Museum.

The Northwest Library in Reno, Nevada, has a Holocaust section, from which I borrowed and read many books about Jews in Shanghai. The United States Holocaust Museum in Washington, DC, provided a wealth of material from its large selection of books about Jewish Shanghai.

David Kranzler's dissertation *Japanese, Nazis & Jews* is a well-researched study of the events surrounding the Jewish refugees of Shanghai.

Lilian Willen's *Stateless in Shanghai* provided information about her life in Shanghai interwoven with her research on the history.

I also contacted many people. Some willingly shared their stories or those of close relatives. Others still refused, after seventy years, to talk about their time in Shanghai. Among those who kindly shared were Doris Fogel, Al Spokoiny, Lisa Brandwein, Eva Berg, Faith Beckerman, and two others who preferred to remain anonymous.

Early on, I spoke to Mazal Hendeles, whose father was a Sephardic rabbi in Shanghai and learned about prewar life among the wealthy. Rita Eichstein shared her father's experiences; he was one of the fortunate refugees to have come on a Sugihara visa.

During the process of writing the manuscript, Patricia Dicks, Kathleen Reilly-Repass, and Jennifer Joseph offered valuable comments to improve the story.

Jessica Santina did a superb job editing the manuscript. Without the people at Lucky Bat Books, *Shanghai Losses* would have remained on my computer. And a thank you goes to Sarah Katreen Hoggatt for designing the book you hold in your hands.

Every attempt was made to make this an error-free work. If any mistakes survived, I am solely to blame.

Adrienne Tropp,
February 2022

Photo Credits

Cover: *S.S. CONTE ROSSO (Italian Passenger Ship, 1922-1941). Public domain*

Cover: *Rachel. (Photo courtesy of Richard Tropp.)*

Figure 1: Announcement about the Proclamation. (United States Holocaust Memorial Museum, Photo Archives #21604, February 18,1943. Photo courtesy of Eric Goldstaub.) 2

Figure 2: Map of areas of Shanghai, circa 1935. (Photo courtesy of Richard Tropp and Shanghai Jewish Refugees Museum.) 12

Figure 3: View of the Garden Bridge. (United States Holocaust Memorial Museum, Photo Archives #30678, 1939-1945. Photo courtesy of Ralph Harpuder and Peter Witting.) 23

Figure 4: Aerial view of Shanghai, China, mid-1937. (Photo by Harrison Forman, courtesy of University of Wisconsin-Milwaukee Libraries Harrison Forman Collection.) 23

Figure 5: Inside a lilong (lane). (Photo courtesy of Virtual Cities Project: Virtual Shanghai.) 23

Figure 6: House belongings moved by rickshaw, 1930. (Photo courtesy of Virtual Cities Project: Virtual Shanghai.) 40

Figure 7: Playing mahjong, 1930. (Photo courtesy of Virtual Cities Project: Virtual Shanghai.) 43

About the Author

Adrienne Tropp with her guide in
Shanghai (photo by Richard Tropp)

ADRIENNE TROPP is a former teacher who has always
been fascinated by different cultures. She grew up
in the multiethnic city of New York and now resides in
Washington, DC. For most of her tenure as a teacher, she
taught humanities and world literature. Adrienne became
interested in Jewish communities around the world when
she was assigned a Sunday school class on the subject. She
has traveled extensively, including to what was once the
Shanghai Ghetto.

adriennetropp.com